For Sheila

Bill Mann

Carleen Glasser

EVERY STUDENT CAN SUCCEED

William Glasser, M.D.

EVERY STUDENT CAN SUCCEED

William Glasser, M.D.

This book is available through William Glasser, Inc.
22024 Lassen Street, Suite #118
Chatsworth, CA 91311
Phone: 800-899-0688 / Fax: 818-700-0555
Web site: http://www.wglasser.com
$14.00 each - includes postage & handling
Quantity Discounts Available

Photo of Dr. Glasser by
Craig Ferré Photography

Cover Design
by
Dale and Penni Neely

Disclaimer

This document is an original work of the author. It may include reference to information commonly known or freely available to the general public. Any resemblance to other published information is purely coincidental. The author has in no way attempted to use material not of his own origination.

ISBN: 1-58275-051-3

Printed in the United States of America

DEDICATION

To the staff, students and parents of the first Glasser Quality Schools, whose dedication to these ideas has made this book possible:

Aikman Elementary School

Belleair Montessori Academy

Canterbury High School

Horizons Alternative School

Huntington Woods Elem. School

LABBB Collaborative

McFall Elementary School

The Learning Place

Contents

ACKNOWLEDGEMENTS

First and foremost I want to acknowledge the help that my wife Carleen has given from the start to the end of this project. Her meticulous editing, questioning, the title and even some of the cover design, I owe to her.

Since this has been a rush project, when my laptop computer broke in Canada where we had allotted the time to finish the manuscript, three of our associates stepped in and typed for almost three days until the first draft was almost finished. They were Ellen Gélinas, Pat Donihee and Diane Cormier Northrup. Naturally as they typed, they made valuable suggestions and gave us a lot of positive feedback.

A special thanks goes to Al Montgomery, one of our senior instructors located in New Orleans, for asking me to help him answer the important question that frames this book and refusing to take no for an answer. That question, with which I am very familiar, that teachers keep asking him is: What do I do now with the students who disrupt my class while I am in the process of putting your ideas into practice? Al, this whole book is an answer to that question.

It is also necessary that I give credit to Linda Harshman and her staff who work long hours to do what needs to be done to get a book ready for publication. What they do is not easily seen but, believe me, it is there.

Finally, on a very sad note I want to express our personal sorrow and also the sorrow of all in the William Glasser Institute for the sudden death of one of our most supportive people, Larry Palmatier. I have had the pleasure of working with Larry for over twenty-five years and he has been a major source of inspiration and encouragement. I am especially saddened because I so much wanted to share this book with him. His work as a teacher of counseling at the University of San Francisco has impacted so many lives. He will be missed. Our heartfelt condolences go out to his wife, Indira and to his children.

FOREWORD

For over 30 years, Bill Glasser has been writing about the follies of external control in our lives and in our schools. But just when you think he can't possibly top his previous books, he does. In this new book, *Every Student Can Succeed*, he shows how, in a common sense manner, to eliminate failure in schools and to close the gap in student learning where all students learn well.

Most of us in the school business know there is much peer pressure for students not to learn and that just getting by is their goal. We also know that most students are not learning at the competent "A" or "B" level. Our own grading system will attest to this fact. Just look at the percent of students getting A's and B's and those getting C's, D's, and F's. You will probably find that less than 50% of your students are achieving at competent levels.

Bill Glasser addresses these perplexing problems and offers double suggestions to make a difference in the lives of children as well as in the lives of teachers. He challenges us in his usual non-coercive brilliant way to change our practices and to stop doing what we know has not worked. If we truly want outstanding achievement and students to be responsible and want to learn, we must give Glasser's ideas and suggestions a chance to work. I have. While Superintendent of the Johnson City Schools, I observed students achieving two to three years above grade level and most students reaching the competent level of "A" and "B". At the same time, absenteeism and discipline problems declined.

Everyone who works with students, who wants to see schools get significantly better, or who prepares new teachers should read this book carefully and then put Glasser's ideas into practice. Having knowledge alone is not power, using knowledge is. The practice and skills presented will truly transform your schools to highly achieving, caring ones. Furthermore, students will thank you for making the changes, helping them to be responsible, and allowing them to achieve at highly competent levels.

—Dr. Albert Mamary, President
Renewal for Better Schools and
former Superintendent
Johnson City Schools, NY

PREFACE

I think you may be curious why I am writing a new book on education after writing four books previously. The main reason is that with the publication of my book, *Choice Theory*, in 1998, I finally completed a theoretical framework for all I had been trying to do. Since then I've written *Counseling with Choice Theory* the applications of Choice Theory® to counseling; *What is This Thing Called Love?* to the problems of unmarried women; *Getting Together and Staying Together* to the problems of marriage; and *Fibromyalgia* to the problems of sufferers.

All of those books are published by HarperCollins except for *What is This Thing Called Love?*, and *Fibromyalgia* which you can get from the *The William Glasser Institute*. If you find this book helpful in school and are struggling with any of the problems explained in the books above, you might want to see how Choice Theory can be applied to your personal life.

After visiting four of the Glasser Quality Schools since December 1999, I was so impressed with how they had applied Choice Theory to student success, I decided I needed to write this book and call it, *Every Student Can Succeed*. I believe this is possible because I've seen it happen in these schools. If you follow what I suggest in this book, you can create a Quality Classroom. If your principal can lead your staff the way I suggest here, your school will become a Glasser Quality School.

One

Successful Teaching Is Based On Strong Relationships

In this book, I will share what I believe remains to be said about teaching after working with schools for close to fifty years. Thousands of teachers have read my four previous educational books and followed many of my suggestions. I have kept in close touch with their work and recently there's been a lot of progress. From what they have done, I believe I can now show that any teacher who follows what I suggest in this book can create a classroom in which all students succeed no matter how difficult the students are to teach. A lot of progress can be made the first year. What I suggest will actually take less effort and be more pleasant than what you are doing now.

Any school, led by a principal who supports what is written here and encourages a staff committed to using these ideas, can get a very good start toward becoming a *Glasser Quality School*, or as it will be referred to in this book, a GQS. I could not make this claim until the spring of 2000 when I visited the Aikman School (K-3) in Hereford, Texas, the most recent school to declare itself a GQS. Prior to this, the other seven GQS's were not in low income neighborhoods and all the students spoke English. Aikman is the only one in a low income neighborhood with less than 20% of its 500 students speaking English when they enter.

When I visited Aikman, all the students were speaking English fluently and all had passed the Texas Assessment of Academic Skills test, the TAAS, in English at the 90th percentile or above. It is as successful an elementary school as any in the country. I have always believed that it doesn't matter where the students come from; what I have been suggesting since I wrote *Schools Without Failure* in 1969 could significantly improve any school. But now, with Aikman and with this book, I can safely say that any school can fulfill the criteria for becoming a Glasser Quality School. These criteria are:

1. Relationships are based upon trust and respect, and all discipline problems, not incidents, have been eliminated.
2. *Total Learning Competence* is stressed and an evaluation that is below competence or what is now a "B" has been eliminated. All *schooling* as defined in this book has been replaced by useful education.
3. All students do some Quality Work each year that is significantly beyond competence. All such work receives an "A" grade or higher, such as an "A+".
4. Students and staff are taught to use Choice Theory in their lives and in their work in school. Parents are encouraged to participate in study groups to become familiar with choice theory ideas.
5. Students do better on state proficiency tests and college entrance examinations. The importance of these tests is emphasized in the school.
6. Staff, students, parents, and administrators view the school as a joyful place.

Each book I've written has expanded my education ideas and this book is no exception; it has a lot of new material. As I look over all I've written, I wish I could have written this book first because it attempts to provide answers to the questions that teachers have been asking me since the early sixties, such as: I like your ideas but what do I do with the students I'm having trouble with while I'm putting your suggestions into place? While there is new and important theory in this book, it is theory that lends itself directly to practice.

You may have already read or will want to read some of my other books, especially, the 1998 book *Choice Theory,* the theory upon which all my ideas are based. But there is no hurry. This book alone can get you well on your way toward creating your own *Quality Classroom.* It provides you with specific, workable suggestions that should help you deal with almost any problem you may encounter as you teach from kindergarten through high school. Much of it will address things you can do immediately that will prevent problems so that you won't have to worry about them anymore.

In this book, I will talk a lot about the Glasser Quality School (GQS). Essentially this is a school in which all the classrooms are Quality Classrooms, all students are doing competent work and many are doing quality work. Discipline problems have disappeared, state test scores are significantly higher—above the 80th percentile is common—and it is obvious to anyone who enters the school that it is filled with joy. This is a school, you would want to teach in and want your own children to attend. There are now eight Glasser Quality Schools that you can visit and see with your own eyes what they have done. They are listed in Appendix A. I expect there will be more by the end of the year, 2000.

Almost all I suggest you do in this book does not require that anyone change but you. If several of you in a school begin to make these changes, you can help each other and your job will be easier. If your principal supports what you are doing, it will be much easier. But if no other teacher in your school does this and your principal does not support you, you can still be a happier, more effective teacher and move your own class or classes close to what they would be in a GQS.

While this book focuses on practice, it does not ignore theory. In fact, all I suggest that you do is based on choice theory. But I believe the best way to learn choice theory is to put it into practice. Only at the end of the book, when I suggest that you teach choice theory to all your students, will I refer to some chapters in the book, *Choice Theory*, and explain the small amount of this theory you need to know to teach it to your students.

What will make some of the things I suggest difficult to do is that choice theory, unfortunately, is not common sense. Therefore, much of what I will suggest here will not only be new to you, it may go against what you have been taught all your life. At times, it may seem to be exactly the wrong thing to do. On the other hand, because a lot of you may have serious doubts about the effectiveness of much of what you've been taught, you may be more than willing to try something new. Many teachers have told me that these ideas are as welcome as a breath of fresh air.

Ultimately, everything I suggest in this book is based on how you and your students feel and that given a choice, both you and they would rather feel good than bad. Or would rather be happy than sad. This means that when you have difficulty teaching a student, one thing you can be absolutely sure of is that student is unhappy in your class and, very likely, unhappy in school. And if you are unsuccessful in dealing with him, the same could be said of you.

It is no different out of school. If the people in your home are doing what you believe they should be doing, you are happy. If your mate or your children are not doing what you believe they should be doing, you are unhappy. Or to put it another way, if the important people in your life are healthy and behaving even better than you dare to hope for, your life is filled with joy.

Joy is a word not usually associated with what goes on in most of our schools and many of our homes. But it is a word frequently associated with a Glasser Quality School and with homes in which everyone practices choice theory. Joy is the antithesis of unhappiness. I think it is safe to say that no matter how your life is going, unhappiness is the most accurate way to describe it when it is not going as you want it to go. Getting down to basics, the most important human problem, maybe the only human problem, is long-term *unhappiness.*

If you are happy, you'll tend to say to yourself, leave things alone, don't rock the boat. But if you are unhappy, it is almost impossible for you not to think a lot about what you believe is causing your unhappiness. The first things that will cross your mind are: *Whose fault is it that I'm unhappy? Or what's wrong, that's making me unhappy?*

It is possible, but very unlikely, that you will blame yourself for your unhappiness. The more unhappy you are, the more you will try to do something to feel better but it is still unlikely that you will try to make major changes in your own behavior. Most of your efforts will be directed at trying to change someone else. Or you might do something to feel better without dealing with the situation such as running away from it, trying to ignore it or using drugs to blot out how you feel.

If you are an unhappy teacher, the first thing that will cross your mind is to blame your students, principal, parents, or school board. Some or all of these people are not doing what you believe they should do; and you may be justified in wanting them to be different. They may be behaving in ways that are making your job more difficult such as blaming you for your students scoring low on the state achievement tests. But in this book, over and over, I'll be sharing with you what I've finally learned: *The only person you can count on when you are unhappy is yourself.* This is why, everything I am going to suggest is something you can do that does not depend on what anyone else does.

This does not mean it's always all up to you to do everything. But what is up to you will be how you deal with the people or things that you believe are making you unhappy. What I will suggest is how to deal differently with the people I just mentioned. If you can relate to them differently, they may start to behave differently and this difference may make your job both easier and more successful. In other words, by dealing with them differently, they may become more interested in doing more for you than they're doing now.

Throughout this book I will strongly suggest that if you want the help of other people, you may have to consider stopping some things you have done all your life. Even if these things seem right to you, it may be that doing them is harming your chances of getting help or cooperation from other people.

For example, I call these harmful things we do as we work with other people, things that seem so right at the time we do them, *the seven deadly habits that destroy relationships.* I'll mention them here but I'll get into them in more detail throughout this whole book. The deadly habits are: *criticizing, blaming, complaining, nagging, threatening, punishing and rewarding people to control them.* Most people use them so much that they don't think about how deadly they are to the relationships they need.

Since almost all the problems you encounter in school are caused by unsatisfactory relationships with your students, other teachers, parents and administrators, throughout this whole book I'll stress the importance of good relationships. As explained by choice theory, human beings are social creatures. The need to get along well with each other, to go so far as loving each other is built into our genes. To be happy, we have to figure out how to gain and maintain good relationships with the people in our lives. When we are unhappy, almost always it is because we have failed to do this.

It's not that many people in our lives go out of their way to treat us badly. But we make a mistake if we predicate what we do with them on how they treat us; for example, if you treat me well, I'll treat you well. I know what I am saying doesn't seem fair to you but, if you depend on the fairness of others for your happiness, your life will be filled with disappointment.

What I'm trying to tell you is that, in the end, the only person you can count on is yourself. I'm sure this isn't something you like to hear. It makes life seem so unfair. But difficult as it may be, there is a real plus in depending on yourself. Because when you do, you have a lot more control over what happens to you; the more you depend on others, the more they have control over you. But even though you can't control other people, I'll suggest many things you can do that will lead others, such as your students, to do what you want.

For example, if in instances before you read this book you would have used a deadly habit with an out-of-order student, and you stop using it, you may find that the student quickly calms down and follows directions. All he was used to was your use of the habits and because of your use of them, you and he have had a very bad relationship. Just stopping the habits one time, especially when he expects you to use them, can make a big difference. I'll get into some detail later on how to do this.

A further plus about this book is that everything I suggest will either help you make your relationships better or leave them where they are. Nothing I'll suggest will make anything in your life worse; using my suggestions is risk-free.

To explain this a little more, think about all the people in the world who are trying to make other people do things they don't want to do. You are far from being the only one who doesn't seem to be able to control other peoples' behavior. Essentially, you are all asking the same question I posed at the beginning of this chapter: *How do I get more people to do what I want them to do?*

Business owners are asking, how do I get my customers to buy more? Politicians are asking, how do I get more people to vote for me? Network executives are asking, how do we get more people to watch our shows? If the business owners asked me, I'd say, make a better product at a price your customers can afford. If the politicians asked me, I'd say, figure out a way to get the message across that you're the best person for the job. If television executives asked me how to get more people to watch their shows, I'd say, come up with better shows and less advertising. What I'd be saying to all of them is you're responsible; don't blame the people you're trying to reach.

But now let's take a look at another three groups asking similar questions. Bosses ask, how can I get my workers to work harder? Parents ask, how can I get my child to do his homework and take more responsibility around the house? Perhaps more than any other group, teachers ask, how do I get more of my students to work hard in school? The questions seem similar but if I answered the same way as I did in the last paragraph, *that it's up to you to do more*, many of you would disagree. You'd tell me, 'It's not up to me. I'm doing all I can. It's up to them to take more responsibility. They're lazy, irresponsible and unmotivated.'

Let's say you're right. The workers, your own children and the students are lazy, irresponsible and unmotivated. What makes them so different from customers, voters and television viewers? The difference is clear. You accept that the customers don't have to buy anyone's products; the voters don't have to vote for the politician, they don't even have to vote; the viewers can watch other programs or not watch at all. There is nothing anyone can do to make these three groups do what others want. Basically, no one has control over them.

But if you are a boss, parent or teacher, you don't accept that you have no control over your workers, your children or your students. The society in which we live has preached forever that we do have control over workers, children and students. Further the society has told you: *If you can't make the workers work, children obey and students study, it's your fault for not forcing them to do it.* The society tells you in no uncertain terms to use the deadly habits, especially to punish. A few people suggest rewards or maybe a little carrot first before a lot of stick.

The interesting thing is that while parents and teachers have mostly remained the same, recently some bosses have changed. In the good old days they used to threaten workers with no raises and, if they still didn't buckle down, fire them. Now they complain, I can't fire them, there's no one to replace them. So they are starting to pay workers a little more and treat them slightly better. My guess is treating them better is as important in keeping them as paying them more.

But what I hear from both parents and teachers is: *No matter how much I threaten and punish, they still won't do what I tell them. Sometimes the situation gets worse.* As "right" as they may seem, the seven deadly habits don't work. What I am asking parents and teachers in this book is, "Would you consider changing the way you teach?" But as soon as I even suggest they change, many of them will say, "There's nothing wrong with what I'm doing. I do it for their own good and they don't appreciate it. There's something seriously wrong with their brains. You're a psychiatrist, I think they need some kind of medication."

It's at this point that I differ with many psychiatrists and pediatricians who are now medicating millions of young students. More and more in the past twenty years, pediatricians and psychiatrists have agreed with the teachers, and often the parents, saying there is something wrong with these children's brains that can be fixed by medication. This is exactly what many teachers and parents want to hear. It assures them there is nothing wrong with the way they teach or parent. So now we have an epidemic of kids with "damaged brains." In affluent school districts where parents can afford professional "help" and prescribed medication, as many as 25% of students are on brain drugs to make them pay attention and sit still.

If you believe you can't teach many of your students unless some psychiatrist or pediatrician puts them on strong brain drugs, you will be disappointed in this book. I, as well as many other psychiatrists, don't think there is anything wrong with the brains of children who don't pay attention or don't sit still in school.

I will suggest what you can do with these students so they will decide to pay attention, sit still and do competent work. There is some research[1] that indicates strong brain drugs will make them sit still and seem to pay attention. But no research shows these children doing significantly better schoolwork.

I can take you to Glasser Quality Schools populated by students just like yours where all the children pay attention, where there are no discipline problems and where the students are scoring very well on the state achievement tests. These schools are not doing anything miraculous. They are using the ideas I will suggest here, ideas you can use and get the same results.

What we call ADD, ADHD or ODD is the way children who have unsatisfying relationships with you and other adults in their lives choose to behave in schools. There is nothing wrong with these children's brains. What is wrong is that teachers are attempting to force them to do things in class that they don't want to do before these teachers have made a strong enough relationship with the students, and changed the way they teach, enough to convince the students that the work is worth doing. Very few of them work in school because they think an education is valuable for them. They work for you because they like you and because they see the sense in what you are trying to teach.

Until we can relate better to our students and explain why what we are asking them to learn is worth learning, they will continue to behave in ways that are described by the diagnoses above. These, often gifted, children are especially sensitive to the deadly habits, and it is wise to avoid using the habits with them no matter what they initially do in class. I'll get into how to do this later in the book. None of what I'll suggest is easy but it's a lot easier than what you're doing now. The payoff for this effort for you is the happiness that comes with success. For them it is both the happiness of connecting with you and the joy of learning.

Hard as it may be for you to believe, these students are really no different from you or anyone else in the world who is forced to do what he or she doesn't want to do by someone they may not like. They resist. The more unhappy they are, the more they resist; and the more they resist, the more you will be tempted to use the habits on them; and the more you do that, the worse things will get. But I can tell you from experience that, as soon as you can create the relationship they need with you, they change very quickly for the better.

Research shows that these are usually students who are well above average in intelligence[2]. Once you get them on your side, they become very good students.

The answer to these problems is not drugs. It is you giving up the habits that are destroying your relationship with them. Satisfying relationships are at the core of the huge success that can be seen in the schools that have now moved to using these ideas.

While giving up the coercive habits will greatly improve the way you and your students relate to each other, later in the book I will also explain a new way to *teach*, *test* and *grade* that I call the *Competence Based Classroom* or *CBC*. In the CBC, the students learn why they need to learn what you teach and also learn that they can have much more control over what they do than they ever had before. The more students have control over their learning, the harder they will work. Once you give up the habits and get CBC's working for you, all you have to do is relax and enjoy teaching.

The good news is that everything I suggest you do in this book works best with the students who are now the most difficult to teach. This way of teaching will reduce the present educational gap between the rich and the poor, which eventually may reduce the widening economic gap between the haves and the have-nots. Keep in mind that the success of any human endeavor—learning in school certainly included—*is directly proportional to how well the people involved in the endeavor get along together*. Helping you achieve this in your school, is the goal of this book.

Two

The Problems Inherent In the Present ABCDF Grading System

I believe our current use of the ABCDF grading system is the cause of many students refusing to work in school. In this chapter, I'll explain what's wrong with this system and recommend it be abandoned. Later in the book, when I describe the Competence Based Classroom in detail, I'll explain how the flaws of the current grading system can be avoided in Glasser Quality Schools.

As long as we use ABCD and F's, we have little chance to improve our low-performing schools in which C, D, and F grades are endemic. It is tragic that our disadvantaged students who, in this new century, desperately need to graduate from high school with a transcript that certifies competence, are trapped in a system that works for less than 20% of them.

For many students, as long as they graduate, a C and D education, is socially acceptable. I'll also admit a diploma is a plus when students look for work. But in the year 2000, if they are educationally unprepared for the job they get, they won't be able to keep it. Therefore, for the short term, there is still some good in this system. But for the long term, as we move further into the new high-tech information society, we will be faced with a serious problem. Only the A and B students will be prepared for work or college. As hard as teachers try to prepare the disadvantaged students, this grading system will frustrate their efforts.

In our new society, using low grades to give credit for incompetence doesn't make any sense. Diploma or not, already almost every student needs a competent education for success in life. In schools with a majority of disadvantaged students, graduation has been almost completely separated from competence. While we are still urging disadvantaged students to come to school, we then give many of them a piece of paper that doesn't reflect competence to the level needed in the modern world.

By separating graduation from competence, we are perpetuating two false and very destructive educational ideas. The first and worst is that a high school education is not worth very much. Some high schools in affluent neighborhoods are not far from moving into a situation where all high school credits except AP credits are tainted as less than competent.

With the rise of the AP system, the schools for the disadvantaged are even worse off as they offer very few AP classes. What we actually have right now is a two-tiered school system: AP, A, and maybe B students are competent. The rest are not. We have enough separation as it is between the rich and the poor in our country without using our schools to widen the gap. We need more schools like Aikman where the gap has been completely eradicated.

The second and equally destructive, widely held belief is that huge numbers of students are not capable of learning enough to do competent work, such as, earning a B in every course. Teachers, when they see students graduating who have never earned a legitimate B in their school career, find it hard to believe these

16

students are capable of doing more. The worst part is that many of the students who have never done competent work also believe they are incapable of doing it.

About ten to fifteen years ago, some people in disadvantaged neighborhoods began to question this general perception that so many students were incapable. They said, "It's not the fault of the students that they haven't learned very much; it's the fault of the schools for graduating students who can barely read, much less write and calculate." But no one, as far as I know, points the finger at a major culprit, the ABCDF grading system.

Instead, what has happened is the sudden and overwhelming creation of a second non-ABCDF evaluation system, the state achievement tests. The results of these tests show clearly there is no correlation between C's and D's and competence. In the disadvantaged neighborhoods, there isn't a very high correlation between B's and competence. I believe the state tests are a needed addition in that they clearly show the flaws of the ABCDF system. Still no one in power has come out and said what needs to be done: get rid of the ABCDF system.

Recent results (2000) on the Stanford 9 test in California show that the elementary students are scoring higher. These students are benefiting from the new, and much smaller classes where they can relate better to their teachers. With this improved relationship, they don't mind their teachers pushing them to do more work. By looking at the results, however, there is an indication that in some schools the students have been pushed too hard and this has been counterproductive.

But I think this tendency to push too hard will be recognized and I suspect almost all the elementary students' test scores, many abysmally low, will keep rising. Also many elementary schools do not use the ABCDF grading system as rigorously as it is used in middle schools and high schools. They have gone over to the second system, a test like the Stanford 9, which is more accurate and that helps. Also from a statistical standpoint there is plenty of room for improvement in most schools so this makes improvement more feasible.

But I, along with many others, question whether this elementary school improvement will continue as the students grow older and move into middle schools and high schools. This is because the same push for better performance has not shown any significant improvement in the secondary schools and I believe we will not see any as long as we continue to use the ABCDF system. With this credit-for-incompetence system, we have almost no way within the schools themselves to find out what the low-achieving students are capable of learning.

Secondary school teachers, especially high school teachers, tend to be concerned about graduation rates and making sure their students pass. Once they do, even with a C or D, there is little incentive for many secondary teachers to continue to push for higher performance. The student will say, 'Get off my back, I got a passing grade, what more do you want?' Unless we stop giving school credit for C and D grades, state achievement testing in the middle and upper grades will continue to show little improvement. If we push these students for more, we may start to see less.

But there is another middle school and high school problem that will also prevent state test scores from rising nearly as fast as in the elementary schools. This is the relationship problem I explained in the last chapter. There is almost no chance that secondary school teachers, with a teaching load of a hundred or more students, can create anywhere near as good a relationship with their students, in five hours a week, as the elementary teachers can with less than thirty students all week long. What makes this even more difficult is that the secondary students probably need a good relationship with their teachers as much, and possibly more, than they needed it when they were smaller.

I think by now you can see there is no sense testing for competence on tests like the TAAS or Stanford 9 if we use C and D grades in class. This is a hole in the system you could drive a truck through. But I also recognize we are not about to get rid of ABCDF grades. Even if the teachers wanted to, the affluent parents would not stand for it. If nothing else they want low grades to show how much better their children are than those who get low grades.

What this book will explain later is that any teacher in any school, rich or poor, can teach for competence by using the competence based system despite the flaws of the ABCDF grading system. While I will explain the Competence Based Classroom later, here I want to make this point. The present system does not force a teacher to give C, D and F grades. But before state testing, any teacher who gave only high grades, B's, A's and A+'s would be severely criticized. The public would scream: grade inflation.

But with state testing, any teacher, at any level from first through twelfth grade, could give all high grades and get away with it if the state test scores showed her students were competent. I claim this would happen because it is happening now in the Glasser Quality Schools where all use some variation of the competence based system.

So far what has been found out this year (2000), by the state testing of the high school students, is what the SAT and ACT college entrance tests have been showing for years. High school achievement is directly related to affluence; the correlation between family income and test scores on the SAT is 1.0. In fact, when a California State Test that required much more thinking than the Stanford 9 was given a few years ago, it showed something nobody wanted to see: students with good grades from affluent neighborhoods did poorly, too. There was a lot of pressure from parents and teachers in affluent schools to dumb down the tests and quickly the state spent millions of dollars and did it.

Now in California, we have in the parents' minds an almost perfect test, the Stanford 9, which shows the affluent schools doing well and the poverty or minority schools doing much less well. Instead of blaming the teachers, which they tend to do, the politicians should figure out how to provide the money for the poor schools to have what is now taken for granted in the rich schools: smaller classes at all levels, better materials, books and computers, and clean functioning facilities.

But unless all students can be persuaded to work for competence, which means eliminating almost all C and D grades for credit, it is unlikely that the schools in low income neighborhoods will get the financial support they need. It's a catch 22; you need more financial support to do better but until you do better, you can't get this support. All this is even more reason for teachers in less affluent neighborhoods to go ahead and try the CBC, an important new way to teach especially in middle school and high school which does not cost a penny more to implement. Later in this book, I'll explain the Competence Based Classroom in great detail.

Three

Getting Rid of External Control Psychology

Years ago, when I asked my mentor, Dr. G.L. Harrington, what clients have to do to get help from a counselor, he answered, "Just be there; the rest is up to us." In my experience, it's the same for a Glasser Quality School; all the students have to do is show up. Our job is to do the rest. No matter their family backgrounds, I believe we can convince just about every student who comes to school to do competent work.

The way to do this is by making an effort to connect with them, especially when they give us problems. When the problem students see others like themselves getting along well with their teachers, they begin to think: *this may be something I ought to consider. It may be a lot more fun than what I'm doing now.* You don't have to ask the students in a GQS if they like their teachers or if they like school. You can see the joy on their faces as soon as you walk inside.

Creating this joyful, cooperative environment is not luck. The schools that have done it know exactly what to do and they do it all day long. What they have done is change the way they relate to the students so they get closer to them, individually and as a group. In the words that I will use over and over in this book, *they connect.* They do this by moving from what I explain is an *external control* environment, which destroys student-teacher-classroom relationships, to a *choice theory* environment, which connects teachers, students and parents.

External control is a short, accurate way to describe what happens when we use the seven deadly habits: criticizing, blaming, complaining, nagging, threatening, punishing and rewarding to control, in any situation where we want to get along better with another person or people. Actually there are a few more deadly habits but if you can stop using the ones listed above, you need to have little concern about your relationships with your students, no matter who they are or where you teach. The habits are external and controlling because you, who are outside of your students, are using them to control your students.

For reasons explained in *Choice Theory*, I claim that external control is the psychology all people in the world tend to use when they have difficulty getting along with other people. Teachers use it on students, students use it on teachers and most often both use it on each other. The problem with this universal psychology is that it harms the relationship between people whenever it is used. If continued, external control will destroy every relationship in which it is employed.

What I strongly suggest is that you stop using these habits, not only in your classroom but also at home. Try not to use them on your mate, your own children or anyone else who lives with you. As soon as you do— this can happen in days—you will start getting along better with everyone. If you can remove external control from your whole life, you will be even better off. But when I ask teachers to consider teaching without the deadly habits they say, "But here's this kid disrupting my class. What am I supposed to do, just ignore him and let him wreck what I'm trying to do?"

Absolutely not. You don't ignore him. As soon as he starts his routine, I suggest you begin to relate to him using choice theory from that point on. Instead of threatening or punishing, use the seven connecting or choice theory habits: *caring, listening, supporting, contributing, encouraging, trusting and befriending.* While your use of them is still external to the student, *your attempt is to get closer to him, not control him,* which is a huge difference.

Students who give you a hard time or don't attend, have already chosen to separate from you. That's why they're disrupting. If you can't connect with them, they'll give you a hard time all year, resisting your direction, which is their way of trying to control you. A favorite trick of resistant students is to keep disrupting your teaching until you start to threaten and punish. When you do, they have gotten control of you and can now blame everything they're doing on you. These students are well acquainted with external control; they've struggled against it for years. Only by stopping its use in the classroom, can you begin to interest them in behaving in the way you would like them to behave.

I realize what I am going to show you how to do now will not be easy. I also realize it may not work the first time you try it. The student may taunt you into giving up and going back to what he understands: the threats and punishments of external control. But I am absolutely sure what I will now explain is not only the best thing to do, it is the only thing that has a chance of turning a student around. Also, in a GQS, a teacher does not have to put up with disruptive behavior. If you cannot convince the student to cooperate, you can send him from the class.

What I will now explain involves a thirteen-year-old boy, Tom. What I do with him could be done with any student from elementary to high school. Only the language will change. Although I'll show you two ways to work with Tom, these are not the only things you could do. Once you catch on to the basic principle, get rid of the external control and get closer to him by using choice theory, you can use many different approaches with students like Tom. You will only be limited by your own creativity.

In the first situation, Tom has started to hum and keeps humming to the point where he has the attention of the whole class. But they are also paying a lot of attention to you to see what you're going to do about it. They enjoy the little war that is unfolding between you and Tom and many are rooting for Tom to win. For a while you try to ignore him but it hasn't worked.

What I will suggest to you in both this instance, and also the next one, is to stop what you are doing (i.e., literally stop the class) and say, "Tom, I'm having trouble teaching with what you're doing. I'd like to talk with you for a few minutes. Will you come over here and sit near me?" (Have an empty chair by your desk.) "Or would you prefer I come talk with you there?"

If you have to go over to him, roll your chair to him if it has wheels or bring a chair over. But wherever you talk with him, don't stand above him, sit comfortably beside him. You know what you are going to do and, if you do it, it is unlikely Tom will win this small war. Tell the rest of your students to go back to work but don't be concerned if they stop and listen. What you are going to do is as much for their benefit as it is for Tom.

They'll learn a lot more in the next few minutes about getting along with people than they will from the history lesson Tom interrupted. Tom will quickly calm down because of all this attention. He won't know what to say, so in the beginning you'll have to do most of the talking.

Start by saying, "Tom, I'm concerned about you. I don't think you're happy in here. I'd like you to be happier. I think if you were happier you wouldn't have started to hum. What do you think?"

Tom is surprised and disarmed by this approach in which I start right out by expressing concern for his happiness. He expected what he usually got when he misbehaved, i.e., threats and punishment. Any time you use choice theory language when someone expects external control language, will almost always get his or her attention. This is because the change in approach, choice theory instead of external control, suddenly stops the disconnection that in this case has been going on between you and Tom for a while. Tom will actually feel it stop and may even begin to feel a little closer to you.

He might say nothing or say, "I'm okay, don't worry about me."

This is a weak effort to defend his humming and to say to you that he doesn't need you to care about him. He expects you to continue to talk about the humming but that first mention is all you need to do. Later you might ask him to sit quietly but don't connect it with the humming. He'll make that connection; you don't have to do it. But keep in mind he does need you and a connection with you is the only thing that has a chance to get him to do something in history. Since he doesn't do anything in your class, he expects you'll give him a low grade, which also turns him off. Later in the book I explain the Competence Based Classroom approach in which Tom could get a good grade in history, and this success will help.

But he's wrong about not needing you. He does need you. He is a lonely disconnected student who needs a connection with a responsible adult and by saying what you did, you started this connection with him. You might go ahead and say, "I'm worried about you. If I weren't worried about you, I wouldn't be taking this time to talk with you. You're a smart kid. I'd like to help you get some work done in this class. I think you'd feel a lot better if you did some work."

"I hate history. It's boring. Who cares about that old stuff, anyway?"

"See, that's exactly what I wanted you to say. You're asking a good question. Why should anyone care about history? But tell me, Tom, I teach history. I care about history. But I care about you, too. I don't know what to do. But I know one thing, I'm not going to yell at you or threaten you. I've decided not to do that anymore. If I keep doing that we'll never get along and I'd like to get along with you better. Do you have any suggestions as to what I should do now?"

At this point, Tom may not say anything or he may say something smart like, "Just send me to the office, you're going to anyway." or, "I wasn't doing nothin', you're always picking on me."

But whether he says nothing or either of the above, your job will be to continue to talk with him and avoid using any external control. You might say, "I want to do something that helps you to do better in my class. Look, you don't have to do anything right now. You can just sit there. I'm not going to try to make you work. But I'd like to think about your question and we can even have a little debate in here with the kids who like learning history vs. the kids who don't. I'd like to hear what you have to say. But right now, I'd like to get back to teaching. Could you just sit quietly until the period's over?"

Tom and the whole class have heard what you said. You did not use any external control. You even gave him a choice not to do the work if he didn't want to. But you did ask him not to disrupt for a while or until the period ended. Suppose he keeps disrupting. I assume in your school you can send a student to the office if he refuses to stop disrupting, or send him to another teacher in the school with whom you've made a mutual arrangement. If Tom continues to hum, you need a place to send him and the principal's office is the usual place.

Tom is frustrated by your failure to use external control so as soon as you go back to teaching, he starts the humming again. To be consistent in your attempt to use no more external control, you would have also told your principal that, when you send a student to the office, it would be best for your relationship with that student if she does nothing with him when he gets there. You don't want her to punish him or threaten him, just let him sit there. Later I'll explain how you might help to set up a room or area in your school called *The Connecting Place* for students like Tom. But here, with no such place, you just send him to the office or some other pre-arranged place so that you and the rest of your students will not be disturbed.

The main thing is to keep on good terms with your principal. You don't want to burden her with any more work. She'll like the fact that you don't turn the problem over to her to solve and that she doesn't have to do anything with Tom except let him sit there. Unless, of course, he is so disturbed that he's violent. Then she would follow the school policy for this behavior and contact his parents. Tom's behavior is just disruptive to your teaching. You've already told your principal that as soon as you have some free time, you'll come to the office, get Tom, take him to your classroom and talk with him further.

Later I'll go into detail as to how to do this whether he's in the office or in The Connecting Place. For now let's pick up on what to do if Tom continued to hum. Again stop the class and say,

"Tom, I can't devote any more time right now to this problem. I know it won't help you but I'm sending you to the office. All you'll have to do is sit there. If you sit quietly, I don't think the principal will even ask you why you're there. When I have a free moment, I'll come and get you and we'll talk. Just take this card and give it to the woman in the office and she'll tell you where to sit."

At this point he might say, "I'm sorry, I'll stop humming. Give me another chance." But once you've made up your mind to send him to the office, stick to it. Both he and the class must learn that, while there may be second chances, you don't usually give a second chance in a situation where you've already put up with a lot of humming and finally asked him to stop. He hasn't complied and hasn't even tried to talk seriously with you even though you've given him every chance.

From your talk with him, he's also learned there is no longer any punishment besides removal. There is no low grade for the day or detention. Actually, you didn't use any of the seven habits. You tried to talk with him, you offered him help with his unhappiness, you asked for his opinion about that help, allowed him to sit quietly if he didn't want to work, and he chose not to. You have already arranged that the principal won't reprimand any student you send to her so there will be no punishment in the office.

I suggest that for a few minutes after Tom leaves you might talk to the whole class. Tom's behavior, no matter what he did, is not that important. What's important is that the whole class be involved and, of course, they already are involved. Later in this book, as you move further toward a GQS, I will suggest you work toward giving the whole class more responsibility for what's going on including helping with students like Tom.

As soon as he leaves, get the class together and ask them for their opinion of what you did with Tom. Ask them how they might have handled it. Ask them if they noticed you were really trying not to send him to the office. Ask for advice on how you can handle him when you see him later in the day. Explain to them you are going to give up threatening and punishing everyone and you'd like their help to make it work.

Now let's take the same boy Tom, in a similar situation, but show how it could work out differently. Tom has been clowning around in the back of the room with Jeff and given Jeff a push. Jeff has faked the severity of the push and chosen to fall out of his seat with a crash. He's obviously not hurt so you don't have to worry about him. The whole class is watching to see what you are going to do. Again, you stop the class and talk to Tom. You can tell the class to keep working but, as before, you don't care if they listen. Listening to what you say can be instructive.

You keep an empty chair near your desk to talk to students for a lot of different reasons that have nothing to do with unacceptable behavior so you just say, "C'mon over here and sit down, I think it'd be a good idea if we had a talk."

Tom comes over and sits down. He swaggers a little; he likes the attention he's getting from everyone and he's confident he can handle whatever you're going to say. You begin with no threat in your voice, just a calm matter-of-fact tone by asking a question. It's good to start the conference with a question because you're immediately trying to connect. It's so much better than starting in with a disconnecting threat.

"Tom, I'm having a little problem, would you help me with it?"

Tom is not prepared for this approach and says nothing. He just looks at you which gives you the signal to go on. You say, "I'm a pretty good teacher but I guess I'm not smart enough to figure out what to do with you after what just happened. I wonder if you could help me?"

Tom knows what he did and what Jeff did and he knows you know it wasn't an accident so he'll try to wiggle his way out of it by blaming Jeff. He won't make any attempt to respond to your question, which you don't let bother you, because all the question was aimed at doing was to get the conversation started without using any external control. You didn't expect him to answer it.

He says, "I didn't do nothin. Jeff was faking. You saw it. What do you want from me?"

"I want some help. I can't teach with this kind of thing going on."

This is still a holding pattern. But it again suggests you want him to stop without any threat as to what may happen if he doesn't.

"I told you, I didn't do nothin. It's not my problem. It's Jeff, talk to him."

You have to keep talking to Tom. Don't even intimate you are going to give up on him and start talking to Jeff. And don't get into whose fault it is. Faultfinding is external control. It doesn't matter so much what you say. You're trying to make a connection and you're avoiding blaming and threatening, kind of keeping on neutral ground. Just to keep the conversation going you say, "I may talk to Jeff later but I've been wanting to talk with you for a long time and, when you gave Jeff that shove, I thought this'd be a good time for us to get together. Jeff isn't hurt. He's fine. I'm worried about you."

"I just touched him. I didn't shove him."

"Tom, I'm not worried about what just happened. You're both okay. I'm worried because as hard as I try, I don't seem to be able to teach you very much. I don't know what to do. I worry when a smart kid like you doesn't want to learn."

Again he says, "History is boring. Who cares about all that old stuff?"

Finally, he's paying attention to the only thing that will help him, improving his classwork, and he's admitted he's not doing anything. It's not clear how you'll reach him but now you've told him you want him to continue to talk with no intimation that you're going to do anything more. The way you put it, it's as if it's your fault he's not learning. But you also had a chance to say he's a smart kid and could do more.

You say, "I can't make you care about history. I can't make you care about anything. But I care a lot about teaching you, and I care about you."

"What do you mean, you care about me? Nobody in this school cares about me."

This is what you hoped he'd say or intimate in some way. The idea of you caring about him has registered. You want to use this opportunity to back up what you just said.

"I'm talking to you because I care about you. You didn't hurt me when you shoved Jeff. You didn't even hurt Jeff. But ever since this class started, I think you've been trying to tell me that I should give up on trying to teach you. I hate to give up on a student as smart as you are."

"You're not going to punish me?"

"Do you want me to punish you?"

This is another non-threatening question asking him to take some responsibility for what he's doing here. He wants to push all the responsibility over to you and then blame you if you punish him. Don't play that game with him, just keep quiet.

He says, "If you're not going to punish me, what are you going to do?"

He's a little puzzled, but he's given you an opening to get off the punishment routine.

Say, "Tom, all I can do is talk to you to see if you'd be willing to do a little more. You said, you don't care about things like history. Would you be willing to write down on a test tomorrow why history is boring to you and what we could do in here to make it more fun? I'll give you credit for anything you write. I'd like to hear from anyone else in the class who has any ideas as well. I want everybody to do well in history."

By now the period is almost over. You took about five minutes away from the class with Tom but it's been time well spent. The whole class was listening very carefully when you said you cared about him and inferred you care for everyone and, also, care very much that they learn. Most of all you want their opinion on history. Maybe you haven't asked very many of them for their opinion on what you teach. Asking Tom instead of *telling* Tom infers you respect him and all of them. You got a lot accomplished by spending five minutes with him, at the end of the period, with the class listening to you very carefully and hearing no external control.

You don't know if he'll write anything tomorrow but you've made a little connection and you've steered the conversation around to schoolwork. He knows the period is almost over. He'll go back to his seat and wait for the bell. As it rings, you might go over to him and say, "I enjoyed that talk. I hope we can keep talking."

He won't say anything. He'll just leave the room. But there is a good chance that this non-punitive, flexible talk has given you a start on the relationship you need to create with Tom if he is to have any chance in school. And you improved your relationship with the whole class. There are ways to make history more interesting like the test question you suggested. If you teach history to students like Tom, whatever you can do to make it more interesting is worth doing.

It's not that this short conversation is going to turn Tom into a new student. But it has a chance of reaching him because, for him, it might be a first. All you can do if you want to teach students like Tom successfully is refuse their invitation to go to war with them. He knows you can always punish him. He's prepared for punishment. What this book will teach you is to avoid punishment so he can't blame you for his problems. By trying to get close and not punishing, he may begin to think that if you care about him, maybe he ought to care about himself and maybe it might be a good idea for him to do more. He can't get any satisfaction out of blaming you anymore because there's really nothing to blame in what you've done.

In either situation, you might make it a point to greet him at the door and have a few pleasant words with him the next day. He knows he can repeat yesterday's performance and push you to the point where you will have little choice but to send him to the office. But in this situation, he also knows that you rejected his invitation yesterday and this has given him a chance to choose some better behavior today.

If a lot of the students take you up on your invitation to tell you why they don't like history, you might have them write on this for about twenty minutes and then try to get a class discussion going on the question. Even if Tom or Jeff, the two trouble makers in the class, haven't written anything, you might persuade them to say something in the class discussion. If they do, it might also be a first for one or both of them.

I know that you may be thinking, 'This won't work. The whole class will rebel if I let Tom get away with what he did. I'll lose control; it'll be a disaster.' But you didn't have control in either instance or he wouldn't have done what he initially did. Think of the unhappy students like Tom whom you're attempting to teach. The more you find out about their lives outside of school, the more you realize they are barely connected with their natural parents, stepparents or any adult. Knowing this, you need to be careful not to send messages home telling their parents about things they did wrong in school. That kind of message is likely to get them punished at home. Believe me, there's little choice theory in Tom's house.

His parents already believe he's a trouble maker. Any support you give to that belief may harm what little connection he may have at home. The only adult Tom has who wants to connect with him may be you. And you're the only one who can connect with him enough to convince him to pay attention in school.

When you think about students like Tom, there are moments you feel you'd like to do something for them. It may cross your mind that he desperately needs what your own children have. But you can't take him home. Even if you could, it wouldn't work.

What you can do if you can connect with him is become a very powerful positive person in his life. As soon as he has a little success, you can send a message home telling of his progress. This positive message to the home of a thirteen year old boy like Tom may be the first good news from school his parents have received since he was small. When his mother gets this message she may make an effort to reduce the external control she is adding to his life at home.

Think of Tom as a good piece of furniture well worth making the effort to restore. It's a lot of work but if you are willing to do the work, it will pay off. But unlike Tom, the piece of furniture has no stake in what you are doing. Tom has a big stake in your willingness to make the effort it's going to take to reach him.

If you succeed, he has a much better chance for a happy life. But so do you. It'll not only make your life easier, it'll make it more interesting. When students self-destruct, so many of them do it the same uninteresting way, almost like photocopies of each other. But when they start to pull themselves together as Tom can choose to do if you eliminate all external control when you begin working with him, that process has much more variation. It's not only fun to be a part of this change in Tom, it's exciting.

I am well aware that what I have just written seems on paper to be almost too simple, too easy: just eliminate external control and connect with him. You also may be thinking, 'This isn't really hard to understand, if it actually works, why isn't everyone doing what he's suggesting here?' The main reason is that unfortunately, external control is common sense. I know that as soon as you read my first little talk with Tom, you may have said to yourself, 'Something's wrong. Glasser isn't doing anything. This is all too wishy-washy. It can't be right.'

I also know it's going to be hard for you to do what I did. Everything you've been taught to do as a teacher, has told you to put him in his place. If you let him get away with it, as I seemed to do, the whole class will fall apart. But if you can eliminate the deadly habits, it'll be the other way around. At first, you're not going to be comfortable with this. It takes practice to learn.

But there is one thing you can do, actually ought to do, that may help you to be more comfortable with using choice theory: consider changing the way you live your life outside of school. As I suggested earlier, begin by stopping the use of external control with all the important people in your own life.

The only people I won't ask you to treat differently will be your long-term good friends. I won't because, if you think about it, do you ever speak to them harshly? Do you ever criticize or blame them? Would you ever dream of punishing them? They seem exempt from all the deadly habits that come so quickly to your mind in school and so often at home. As you think about how you treat your friends, it will become apparent that what you do with your good friends is almost pure choice theory.

Pay attention when you're with them. You'll see that neither of you use external control except when you are joking. This means you really don't even have to learn anything new. You just have to treat everyone else in your life as you treat your best friends. This sounds simple but believe me it isn't. Your whole life has been immersed in external control.

Another thing you might do is compare the students in your classes to the kind of student you were in college. Most of you came to college classes to learn. Very few of you gave any college teacher the kind of hard time your students seem to enjoy giving you. If your college teachers were kind and caring, you appreciated their concern but you worked hard without it.

The kindness and caring that you appreciated, but did not need, in your college classes, is exactly what is needed by the students you face each day. In fact, some days, especially when you teach students from disadvantaged backgrounds, you may feel overwhelmed by their neediness. You may ask yourself, how can I cope with this? I know it's not enough for me to suggest you be more caring and kind. Most of you are caring and kind. What you need to learn goes beyond caring and kindness.

The first thing you need to learn is, that while it's nice to think we treat all students the same, we don't. The use of external control increases much more rapidly in poor schools than rich ones especially after the students leave kindergarten. It alienates so many students in the disadvantaged elementary schools that the secondary teachers are overwhelmed by their disconnection not only from teachers but from education itself.

The earlier we get rid of external control in all schools the better off we all will be. But getting rid of it early in the poor schools is necessary if we are to have any success, there.

No one can control family incomes. But, if you are willing to learn what I explain in this book, you can change the way you treat your students.

Choice theory teaches that we choose all we do and we are all responsible for the choices we make. This means we choose both our happiness and our misery. No matter how hard we may try, we can't make another person happy. And it's the same for unhappiness; we can't make another person unhappy either. If we are happy it's because we have figured out how to satisfy one or more of five basic needs—*survival, love and belonging, power, freedom and fun*—built into our genetic structure. If we are unhappy it is because one or more of our basic needs is seriously unsatisfied. As much as we may try we cannot disregard our basic needs. They are the underlying source of all our behavior.

If you understand the power of these needs, you can see the dilemma that our practice of external control psychology has put us in. *The dilemma or conflict inside of us is that while we need to be close and connect with each other, our almost universal belief is that we should use external control when we have difficulty getting along with another person.* When this happens, at least one and usually both people suffer as both you and Tom did when he wouldn't stop humming.

But unlike the needs, which are not chosen and must be satisfied or we will suffer, the psychology, be it choice theory or external control, is not built into our genes. As stated, it is a behavior and all our behaviors are chosen. You can, as I am suggesting throughout this book, choose choice theory instead of external control as I suggested you do earlier in the chapter when you approached Tom.

If you continue to give up external control, as I will explain in Chapter Eleven when you visit him in The Connecting Place, he'll begin to change. It will work because what you are doing is satisfying to his need for love and belonging and will feel much better than the external control both he and you have been using unsuccessfully for so many years. Why external control is so universally practiced is explained in the book, *Choice Theory*, and is beyond the scope of this non-theoretical book. Neither you nor Tom has to read that explanation to give it up.

But while we can't make another person happy or unhappy, we can help Tom and all other students to satisfy their needs. This is what the staff at Aikman has done. They have created a choice theory environment in which all the students are easily able to find love and belonging, power, freedom and fun in school and survival, too. If they are hungry they will be fed.

Actually, I became determined to write this book on May 17, 2000 when I visited the Aikman Elementary School (K-3) in Hereford, Texas. During my visit, I could see no evidence of external control in the school. In fact, Charles Lyles, the principal, never uses the word *discipline* because he has found it's an almost totally external control word. Aikman easily passed the Harrington test. All the students who come to school were achieving competence and all they needed to do was just show up.

Four

No Failure In a Glasser Quality School

My first experience working in a school was in 1956, as the psychiatrist for *The Ventura School for Girls*, a California correctional facility in which girls age fifteen to nineteen were locked up. Most of the girls stayed about nine months and attended school at the facility. In my psychiatric training, I had been taught that the cause of their delinquency was mostly due to a poor home environment. None of my instructors had even mentioned school.

But after I got to know the young women, they told me that their troubles in and out of school began early and continued. All they talked about was how much they hated school. From their standpoint, the source of their difficulties was school failure far more than family problems. Before they came to us, almost all of them had failed for years and had about given up on the idea they could succeed in any school. That they did well in our school came to them as a big surprise.

Very quickly I realized they had the intelligence to do well in school. Most could read, write and calculate reasonably well. When I talked with them about their school failure, they admitted they didn't do much schoolwork and were total strangers to homework. They attended erratically and gave their teachers a hard time when they did show up.

When I asked them why they did so well in our school, their answer was surprising. While they had good things to say about the teachers, they explained that the real difference between our school and the schools they attended was, in our school, they couldn't fail. For them, getting rid of failure was a big deal. They told me that it didn't make any sense to goof off in a school where they could only succeed.

In the schools they'd attended, when they didn't work or gave the teacher a hard time, they were immediately threatened with failure and even expulsion. When they still refused to work they were failed and when they continued to smoke in school—they all smoked—they were expelled. Like almost all adolescents who do poorly in school, they were very sensitive to threats. When they were threatened they resisted. It was as if the only way they could show their contempt for the threats was to punish the school by bad behavior and refusing to work. They were dimly aware that they were also punishing themselves but they didn't care.

By failing, they'd show the teacher: *See, you and your lousy school doesn't mean anything to me. Fail me I don't care.* And once they actually failed they said to themselves, 'What's the sense of continuing to try, I'm already a failure.' They explained to me that when you're already a school failure at thirteen or younger, you begin to give up on the idea you can do anything with your life. You're too young for a job, you're angry at everyone except friends like yourself, your parents are starting to reject you, so you hang out. Hanging out means trouble. They also talked about teachers not caring and told me: *Since no one in that school cared about me, why should I care about them.*

In the years I spent at Ventura, I was lucky to have had the opportunity to talk with so many sensitive, articulate young women. I doubt if many teachers have come close to experiencing the devastating school failure that was common to these young women. Very few professionals have ever failed in school. None of us have gotten more than a few low grades. We have no idea what it is to experience constant threats, low grades and failure. From talking with those girls, I can tell you it's awful. It's like draining the humanity out of a young person and then blaming her for being so uncaring about everyone else including, unfortunately, herself.

We rationalize failure by saying it serves them right. They had their chances and didn't take them. It's their own fault they've ended up the way they are. But when you work with them and get to know them, and appreciate how sensitive, talented and even loving so many of them are, you stop thinking in stereotypes and say to yourself, *maybe we can do something*. And we did. It was simple and sensible and could be done in every school, not just in special schools like Ventura or alternative schools where it is also common. We stopped failing them. We told them we will not fail you and you cannot even get a low grade because we don't give grades.

When we did that, the girls told me that here it's hard for us to convince ourselves that no one cares about us. It was also very hard for them to refuse to do the schoolwork or act up in class. If a new girl would start to act up, the others would have no patience with her. They'd tell her if you don't want to work, keep your mouth shut because we do. If they still continued to act up, the girls would demand that the teacher send them out of the class.

They weren't heroes of resistance like Tom was trying to be when he acted up. They told the girls who acted like Tom that they were fools. This atmosphere is the complete opposite of what so many teachers with whom I work complain about as they see kids all around them resisting like Tom and blaming their behavior on low grades, failure and on teachers who don't care.

Our practice was to lay out the work, teach and explain it and tell them we were willing to help them if they needed help. If they needed more time we would give it to them. But, to get credit they had to do the work competently, something they were quite capable of doing but hadn't done in years. As soon as they did enough to get credit, they could go on to another subject or to a higher level in that subject. School now became open and possible where before it had seemed closed and impossible.

When we talked, they said there should be no failure in any school. As long as there was no failure and they were given more time if they needed it, they accepted that doing the work was their responsibility and they didn't blame us for withholding credit when they didn't work. It was threats that turned them off. The failure convinced them that no one in the school cared about them.

As previously mentioned, we didn't stop with no failure. We refused to give them low grades. Actually we refused to give them any grades. We set a realistic standard of competence. When they achieved that standard, they got credit. It was not a pass or fail system; there was no failure. It was a pass to get credit system and they liked it. We kept no record of anything other than the credit. Many worked hard and some graduated. A few even petitioned the parole board to let them stay locked up in our school for as much as an additional six months so they could gain enough credits to graduate.

In 1969, with their help and advice I wrote the book, *Schools Without Failure*. In that book I pointed out that the girls at Ventura were hardly unique. For every girl in our school, there were ten thousand just like them in the nearby schools. And there were many more boys because boys fail at a higher rate, at all levels, than girls. School failure was a disaster then and it is still a disaster.

Any school system that wanted to do it could do the same thing today we did then. There is no need to record low grades and failure. Banks don't keep a record of the money you don't have. They keep a record of what you have and what you owe. A few of our Quality Schools keep a record of what you need to do to get credit but give no credit until you do it.

I can hear the question going through your mind as you read this. What do we do if the school we teach in makes us give low grades and fail students? We don't have the options you had at the reform school, especially the option to give our students more time. At the end of the year, we have to give them a grade or fail them. The answer to that question is the core of this whole book and every chapter will be devoted to answering it.

There are many things that any school can do besides threaten students with low grades and failure if they don't do the work. These things are all aimed at keeping the relationship between teacher and student strong. You can base everything you do in the school — something no one will stop you from doing — on replacing the external control you have been using, with choice theory.

The use of threats and punishments and even more the daily use of criticism, blaming and nagging turns off everyone but, especially, the students who have not had a positive experience in school. If you have never been in their shoes, it's hard for you to realize how destructive to student motivation the deadly habits are. The students who are doing poorly in your classes are very much like the young women at the Ventura school, capable but turned off. It doesn't matter how capable students are, if they are too angry to work in school.

If you can get rid of the deadly habits and begin to teach differently using the Competence Based Classroom, you will complete what needs to be done. But be patient. The next few chapters will prepare you to use the CBC which will make the external control you have been using, unnecessary.

As I did in the previous chapter, let me again show you how I would deal with a resistant student, a practice I learned years ago while working at the Ventura School, well before I had even a glimmer of the choice theory I've been explaining. It isn't complicated; you could put it easily into practice without knowing anymore than you know now.

Suppose Trevor, a twelve-year-old boy who is not doing his work, challenges you by saying, "What are you going to do if I don't do the work? I don't care if you fail me. This school sucks and so do you!"

When you have to listen to attacks like that, it's pretty hard to think about caring, kindness and connecting. But you can begin to create a relationship with a student who has turned his back both on you and schoolwork by using the following suggestions. Very likely, because of its honesty, you might quickly begin a better relationship with that student.

The first thing I suggest you say is, "Trevor, I'm not sure what I can do for you but failing you isn't it. What's on my mind right now is I want to help you.... Tell me, what good would it do me or you for me to fail you?"

Saying this right out clearly and positively, has a good chance of turning the student's initial accusatory attitude around. He expects you to continue to threaten failure and you're saying, "I'm not even thinking of failing you. I don't want to fail you." Further you admit you don't know what to do when you said, "What good would it do me or you if I failed you?" By removing the threat of failure, you have reduced the power differential between you and Trevor. He now feels he has a chance and if he starts to work he'll find out things are different. He does, in fact, have a chance.

What I'm suggesting works because you are telling the truth. You want to give him a chance. Suddenly, you're much different from most of the teachers he has dealt with who would never admit that it did no good to fail him. It is because you are so different that he may listen to you.

By saying what you just said, you're suggesting that he may have some power to help himself. This is subtle but it's there. You're not saying he has to do anything. You're saying that with you he has a chance to succeed. You want to help him, not fail him. I also think he'll see what you are trying to do is for him, not for you.

This puts him in a little bind. He can't answer your underlying question which is, *Tell me, what good is failure?* He can't because, if he answered it, he'd be defending the value of failure which no student approached this way will want to defend. You are now beginning to build a relationship because it's clear you are on his side. You don't want to fail him; you want to help him.

When he finds it difficult, as he will, to come up with an argument for failure, he won't say anything. He'll just look at you because now you're telling him in clear language, I care about you and this caring is the whole purpose of our present conversation. He can't blame you anymore and, if he still tries to fail, you're going to keep talking to him and offering help.

After waiting a short time, if he still doesn't say anything, you might say any of the following: "I think you can do the work. You may need help. I can even get one of the kids who is doing the work to help you. I'll talk to someone for you if you don't want to ask them yourself. I think you're going to need some more time, so I'll give you more time. We may have to figure out a way for the work to be more interesting. I'll try to do that, too. It'll help you if you do some work at home, but I'll settle for what you're willing to do in school." (Later I'll talk about homework and explain the difference between choice theory and external control homework.)

Later you might say this, "Trevor, if you think of a way to do some more of the work on your own, I'll be happy to listen to your ideas..... But I'll tell you, you and I working together can get this work done. You can't convince me you aren't capable of doing it. Look at all the kids here who are doing well. Are they all smarter than you are? I don't think so." Any control you can give Trevor over his schoolwork will turn out to be very motivating to him.

For most of the non-working kids with whom you are struggling, saying what I just suggested will be a new approach. If you keep talking to Trevor, you'll become a very new person to him: a teacher who talks to him when he isn't working, without using threats. At home and at school, whenever he didn't do what an adult told him to do, all he's heard is what's going to happen to him if he doesn't do it.

I realize this is a one-sided conversation but it is the essence of how to reach Trevor. When you begin to talk to students this way you will develop some new skills that will soon get boys like Trevor to relax and talk with you. It's the seven habits that shut down their willingness to talk. Getting rid of the habits opens them up to the idea that they can succeed.

As I said previously, I'd like to discuss homework. There is nothing in a Quality Classroom that precludes homework as long as you are convinced the student will make an effort to do it. If you know the student won't do it, then when he doesn't, even if you say nothing, he'll still be on the defensive and your relationship with him will be harmed. Often rebellious students don't do homework which is a very common way of challenging your authority.

The best way to deal with homework when you know the students won't do it, is to first make a better relationship with them. Then give them a small amount you know they can do and tell them to work no more than twenty minutes on the assignment. They should just do as well as they can in twenty minutes. If they succeed at this, they may be open to do more.

My experience is that by limiting the time of an assignment that they can do, they may do more than you ask. If they do, in some way, they'll try to tell you they put in extra time. Tell them you appreciate their effort and they needn't worry that you are going to start giving them long assignments from now on. Work out with them what you think is best. They'll now be more open to what you want. Just go slow; this is a sensitive process.

Later when I get into the CBC, you'll see that the separation between homework and classwork mostly disappears. Homework is rarely a problem in a CBC.

To finish this chapter I'd like to tell you something that may interest you: *School failure is not the most widespread accomplishment of external control. It's greatest triumph, by far, is marital failure.* Students don't have anywhere near the fifty- fifty chance of failing that your marriage has. This is why I said earlier that if you embrace choice theory, your whole life has a chance to improve—actually, a very good chance. It seems incongruous to me for anyone to continue using external control at home after you begin to use choice theory in school.

Five

The First Day You Meet Your Class, You'll Succeed

As the teacher, what I have to keep in mind, today and every day is, I'm going to avoid using external control by banishing the seven deadly habits from my classroom. I'm not going to criticize, blame, complain, nag, threaten, punish or offer rewards to try to control my students. I'm going to do this because, above all, I want to create the strong relationships with my students who are the core of a Glasser Quality School.

From the moment I meet my students, I've got to begin differently from the way I've been starting off the year since I first began teaching. On the first day, instead of telling the students what I expect from them, both for schoolwork and behavior, and what I will do if they don't do what I tell them to do, I've got to focus on getting close to them, and really trying to be their friend. If I do what I've always done, I'll be confirming what many of them already believe, and what I believed in a lot of classes when I was in school: that students and teachers are natural adversaries and will never become friends. Friends don't start their friendship the way I've been starting the year talking to my class.

I don't want to start with threats. They're an admission of weakness, an admission that a lot of what I teach isn't very interesting and that I'm worried about losing control. Besides, before I even get to know them, I'm anticipating trouble and telling them that at the first sign of it, I'm going to clamp down.

I've also noticed as soon as I go through my usual *this is what you have to do and this is what's going to happen if you don't do it*, many of my students stop listening. Like I did a lot when I was in their shoes. They've heard it all before. I've seen a few of them frown as if to say, why do I have to listen to this stuff again? I can see that a few are going to be a challenge, the kids who make trouble and never get a good grade, they are already starting to talk, kind of testing me to see how I handle trouble. I'll be on the defensive with them before I even know their names.

Okay, if I'm going to teach differently this year, I've got to start off differently. I'm not going to tell them what they have to do and what I'm going to do if they don't do it. I'm going to start off friendly. I'll say something like, "I think an important part of my job is to do all I can to make sure you have a good time learning. You have to come to school and no one's going to pay you for doing schoolwork. So the least I can do, is make this class fun for both you and me. I think we can learn a lot and still have a very good time."

While they're thinking over what I said, and I don't really expect them to be that impressed even though I think I've caught their attention, I'll ask them some questions starting with, "Are good grades important to you? What grade would you like to see on your report card at the end of the year?" No one will say anything right away but they'll be listening to see if someone else says something. I'll go on, "Does anyone want to see an F or D on your report card? How about a C? How about a B? How about an A? What if the lowest grade you'll ever get in here is a B and if you work hard you can get an A. Who would like to have a year like that with no low grades?"

I'm pretty sure a lot of hands would go up. I'd then say, "I think I've found out a way for all of you to get at least a B in this class. That doesn't mean you can't get an A, but B will be the lowest grade."

Then I'd say, "How about tests? Do you like tests?"

Most of them will say they don't like tests. I'd then ask, "What don't you like about tests?"

By now they would be catching on that I really do want their opinion and for them to tell me all the things they don't like about tests: too hard, too many questions, too much studying, can't remember all the stuff, some kids cheat, don't understand the questions, no good at taking tests, always asking the questions I don't know, never know what to study, and besides...why do we have to take tests, anyway?

Then I could say, "When I was your age I didn't like the same things. How about if I give you a different kind of test. I'd like to let you use the books, your notes, ask anyone in the class for help, ask me for help. All I'm interested in is that you do a good job of answering the questions and when you do, I'll give you at least a B. How does that sound?"

Surely, they'll be skeptical. But they'll still say it sounds pretty good. Then I'd ask them another question, "What did you do all last year when you got a test back from your teacher?" It would take them a while but they'd essentially say, "We threw it away."

I'd say, "Instead of throwing the test away, how would you like to take it home and work on it? Get all the questions right that you got wrong and get a B for doing the work to correct it."

They'd say, "That's cheating. You wouldn't let us do it. No teacher would let us do that."

I'd say, "I will. I'll not only let you do it, I'll even help you or get a student who got them all right to help you. I hate wrong answers but I love it when students correct them and get them right. That's what I'm going to do all this year. How many of you would be willing to correct all your mistakes if I gave you the chance to do it and get a B?"

My guess is all the hands would be up. But if they all weren't up, I'd still go ahead. What I'm offering is hard for them to believe. It's going to take some time for all this to sink in. I'd then say, "I've been talking to you and I'm enjoying it but I think we could arrange the chairs better. In this new way to teach, we're going to have to do a lot of talking. How about if we take a few minutes to rearrange the chairs so it's easier to talk with each other?"

Left to the custodian, the chairs will always be arranged in rows, perhaps, six rows of five chairs. This is the worst arrangement possible if you are to connect with your students, especially, with students like Tom. If you can't get them out of the back seats where you can talk to them easily and naturally, you may never connect with them. Just the activity of getting up and rearranging the chairs with your students is a good, connecting, opening activity.

Right before they get up, you could ask, "Suppose you are sitting around with your friends talking. Aren't you always in some kind of a group like a circle? Could we move the chairs into a circle? Let's each move our own chair when I point to you. One of you can start the circle. Then the rest of you will follow me in this direction (walk to the right) until we've completed the circle."

It gives children a sense of security to experience an orderly move led by a teacher who is obviously interested in trying something new. Then ask them to stand in the center of the circle and suggest a game such as, "Anyone whose birthday is in September sit down anywhere you want."

Then go through all the other months until everyone is seated. They'll finally be able to look themselves over and see that it doesn't make any difference where in the circle they sit, they're all in the front row.

Then you might say, "That'll work fine for all of us talking but how about when we're not all talking, when three or four of you want to sit in a small group to work together and talk to each other. Could we easily change the chairs to small groups of three or four?"

With your help, they then figure out that if we cut the circle at every third or fourth chair, you can make small working groups all around the room. It's easy for them to see they can move from the small groups to the circle and back again. By now you'll be able to say to yourself, I'm beginning to make a connection with almost all of them and none of them seem hostile or against anything that's been going on.

Then you might say, "If we're going to do a lot of talking, what'll we call each other? I'm comfortable with first names. How about if we all use our first names including me. It'll help us all to be friends. I'd like it a lot if you'd call me Bill."

If you aren't comfortable with first names, then don't do it this way but get into a discussion of names. Maybe discuss the idea of nicknames or play a name game to learn each other's names but work something out. I think first names are magical for making the connections that are going to transform many of these students. If I don't use any external control and Tom calls me Bill, it's going to be very hard for him to be disruptive.

This may be enough to do the first day. But this is the mind set for a teacher about to start a Quality Classroom. It is this way of thinking that will make it possible for you to back up what you have been saying about grades and tests by putting the Competence Based Classroom system to work in your teaching that I'll begin to describe starting in the next few chapters. As you do this, more and more you'll see the value of what I'm trying to explain in this chapter.

There's a lot at stake here. You're not just trying to improve their learning, you're trying to raise your students' achievement two or three times or higher than what it has been, especially if they are from a disadvantaged school in a low income neighborhood. A substantial increase has been made in all the Glasser Quality Schools. Aikman School went from the 5th to the 90th percentile on the TAAS.

You may have noticed, I didn't bring up the subject of discipline or what you would do if the students didn't do what they were supposed to do. There are no threats or suggested punishment in what I've explained so far. None of the deadly habits were even mentioned. The better you can build these early relationships, the less problems you will have. Discipline is not a problem in a GQS. It is prevented by good teacher-student and student-student relationships.

Rules are also not needed immediately. As soon as a problem comes up, you might consider a rule but most problems in schools where there are good relationships can be solved with only one—the golden rule. This rule is the basic rule of choice theory. They'll soon discover you are doing a lot for them and they will be more than willing to do a lot for you and for each other. Make an effort to get along with as few rules as possible. The more rules you have the less flexible you can be. Students want to be treated as individuals and too many rules make it hard for you to do this. The more you talk about rules and discipline the more problems you create as students perceive this disconnecting talk as threatening.

The general approach is to replace discipline with an immediate non-external control talk with you as soon as you sense trouble with a student. This often means even before it breaks out you try to spend a little time, talking to him, listening to him, joking with him and injecting a little humor into the situation if you can. A student who has laughed with you will rarely give you a hard time. In a choice theory classroom you are active and involved. As we go into more CBC details, you'll see how this new way to teach builds the strong teacher-student and student-student connections needed for order in the classroom.

Be creative and remember talking to a student about a problem is not brain surgery. If you make a little mistake, you can correct it or apologize for it. In fact, make a mistake in front of the whole class once in a while that is so obvious they'll pick right up on it. As soon as they do, laugh and admit it. Then ask for their help in correcting it. This will give you a chance to show you're human. And, also, it will provide an opportunity to show them we don't learn from making mistakes—we learn from correcting them.

As much as you can, use these ideas in a way that it's enjoyable for you too. Relax, don't be too serious. It's okay to kid around and be funny. Students are the best audience in the world, they are desperate to laugh. You don't have to be a comedian to be a hit in most classes. The more they see you enjoying yourself, the more they'll enjoy themselves, too.

Circle-Ups

As soon as it seems appropriate, introduce them to the idea of *circle-ups*. You've already set up the circle by involving the whole class in a discussion. Now use it to help solve a personal, class or school problem. Refer back to my 1969 book, *Schools Without Failure*, and read the section on class meetings. There isn't a problem that can't be solved if you get them to circle-up frequently. It's a powerful tool that's not used nearly enough. Perhaps the real power of circle-ups is not to talk very much about problems but to prevent them by talking about anything that's interesting. That's what gets them all connected before there is any trouble. They like to talk, they enjoy the attention.

Be sensitive to students who are too shy to talk. Sit next to them in the circle and encourage them. Talk to them individually to plan how they can start to get involved. But don't put pressure on them. Some may sit silently participating little during the whole year yet get a lot out of the circle-ups. Especially, encourage students to bring up some ideas they've learned in school that they have used at home. For most of them, the idea that something they learned in class is useful outside of school will be a new and very positive revelation.

The circle-up is the basic mechanism for all communication, concerns and solving problems. Not usually the first day but soon after, you will run into a discipline problem. This is your opportunity to teach students that the whole class is responsible for helping everyone with problems that arise in class and even out of class. But the class is also responsible for preventing problems in the class and also in the school.

Tell them, if we teach that this country is a democracy, then it is very important that we practice it in our class. A democracy is like a family. People help each other when help is needed, and this class is our family.

Say, "Remember, I could have arranged the chairs myself before you got here but I thought it would be better to do it together. Even though I didn't mention it then, it was a circle-up. Remember, it's your class as much as mine. The more you bring things up the more I'll be able to help you. But one thing I'll try never to do is threaten you or punish you. Threats or punishment make problems, they never solve anything.

Don't worry that circle-ups will take up too much class time. The time spent is worth the effort. It's a powerful communal learning tool which gives students practice in speaking and listening while fulfilling the need for belonging and connection. Just always guard against using external control solutions to any problem. The solution has to be something that brings the problem student and the class closer together. In a circle-up, two or more students can choose to solve a problem they are having before it affects the whole class.

Teach students how it works by explaining that the only person you can control is yourself so each person in the circle-up is responsible for saying what he or she will do to solve the problem regardless of what the others do. Learning this form of negotiating will become a useful, life-long skill for many students.

Keep telling them from the start, as we go along, you'll catch on to the way I teach and you'll learn a lot about the way I am. I'm going to be working hard to learn as much as I can about you. But please remember, school is the place for questions. Don't walk out of this class not understanding what's going on. The worst thing you can do is sit here and not know what you need to know about what I'm teaching.

If you need ten minutes of private time to get close to a student who needs you, use your free period and get permission for the student to be sent to you if she's not in your class. When you see the student, don't think you have to be an expert counselor. Just say to her when she comes, "Look I may be wrong and I'm not trying to poke my nose into your business but when I asked you in class if anything was wrong you said you'd be willing to come see me."

If the student, wants to talk, listen. It is almost certain the problem is she isn't getting along well with someone important in her life; very likely, she's blaming that person for the problem. If she just sits there and seems to be asking you to say something, you might ask a basic question along the same line as, "When you're upset it usually has to do with someone you're not getting along with like a parent or a teacher or maybe another student. Does that information help you at all?"

Either way you will soon get down to the problem relationship. The more sensitive you are to students who need help, the easier your job is going to be. You have chosen the most difficult human relations job there is. Nothing else comes close to what you have to do to create the relationships you need to teach successfully.

Many of the students you teach need you desperately and aren't even aware of how much they need you. They are lonely and very unsure of themselves. If they have a huge personal problem which many have or may have during the school year, that problem will take precedence over their doing schoolwork. You and they working together have the best chance to deal with the problem in school.

If they stop doing their schoolwork, they get themselves into a situation where they fall behind and make the problem, no matter what it is, more difficult to solve. By giving them some early attention, the message you are trying to send them is, I'm your teacher and your friend. Whatever your problem is, if you can make an effort to keep up with your schoolwork, you'll be much better off than if you don't. Remember, even if I can't help you solve your problem, I am an expert on schoolwork. That much I can always help you with.

When I worked at the girls' school, they appreciated that the staff always tried to stand in the way of their choosing self-destructive behavior. When the problem was over (and most problems are gotten over rather than solved) the girl let us know she appreciated our efforts to keep her on track in school.

This is a good approach for all of us to consider when we have a problem. It's difficult to do, but keeping the parts of your life functioning that are not directly affected by the problem is often the key to dealing successfully with the problem. In the context of this chapter, whatever you do or don't do, keep your relationship with your students as strong as you can. If you can do that, you will most likely be able to handle anything that comes up.

Six

The Argument For The Competence Based Classroom

The discipline problems you face in your classroom are caused by students who are not succeeding in school. They know what school success is and they've given up on the idea they'll succeed. Since you're the teacher, they tend to blame you for their lack of success and they're rebelling against you, the schoolwork and the school. The fact that they should work harder doesn't occur to them and won't until they begin to believe they can succeed in school. If you adopt the CBC, they'll discover that school success is possible. That discovery will make a huge difference for the better in their lives.

The CBC turns school failures into school successes. In doing so, it reduces your need to use external control. While I believe I made a good case for reducing your use of external control in the first five chapters, the CBC is by far my strongest argument because, if you put it into practice in your classroom, you won't need external control. Your students will have no reason to rebel against this new way to learn.

There is nothing in the CBC that is hard to understand or difficult to do. While it is more demanding of both you and your students than what you may be doing now, it is so much more successful that I don't think either you or they will complain. It's more likely you'll enjoy it because almost all your students will buckle down and go to work. Also, while it is a new way to teach in school, it is not a new way to teach in the real world. Every successful organization outside of school that depends on teaching, including the armed forces, uses some variation of learning for competence which I'll explain here.

Redefining education and eliminating schooling

In Chapter Ten of *Choice Theory*, I stressed the importance of redefining education. As long as we keep the present definition, *education is acquiring knowledge*–a definition obsolete since books became cheap and easily available–we will fail to improve school achievement. Using this definition, there has been no measurable improvement in the last fifty years no matter how we measure school success. We need to move to a new definition, *education is using and improving knowledge* that is congruent with recent findings on how the brain works and with the information age we have now entered.

Acquiring knowledge leads directly to *schooling*, an education-destroying practice that requires students in academic classes to spend up to eighty percent of their effort acquiring skills and memorizing knowledge they will soon forget or rarely use outside of school; hence, the name, schooling. Think of all the work you did in school, which you knew at the time you did it, you would rarely use outside of school. Unlike school, in the real world, *people are taught to use knowledge*; just acquiring it is insufficient.

For example, as important as it is for a doctor to recognize a disease, what's really important is that he or she uses this information to treat the disease. Or in some cases it's important to know enough not to treat the disease. While it's good to know how to calculate, it's relatively worthless if you don't know when and where to use this skill. I could cite a hundred more examples and so could you. There is no schooling in a CBC. Schooling is an educational disaster.

Most *schooling* is restricted to two common practices: repetitive hand-calculating continuing long after the student has learned this skill, and memorizing facts and formulas that will not be retained and are easily accessible in books and manuals. In many schools, it is considered cheating to use a calculator even after the student has learned to calculate. In almost all schools, it is also cheating to refer to notes or a book to look up facts and formulas on a test when they are needed to solve a problem.

In the real world it is just the opposite. Workers are told to look up what they don't know so they can use it correctly or, if they don't know where to look, to ask, and to use calculators so they won't make costly mistakes. If there is no available calculator, the worker will be asked to have any hand calculations checked by another worker. What is called cheating in school is effective practice in the world of work.

But a more insidious aspect of schooling is when a teacher, after working hard to teach a skill like reading, fails to follow through and teach the student both the value and the joy of using the skill. The success of the Harry Potter books shows that children will read long, complicated books for enjoyment. One reason these books are so successful is because Harry Potter uses magic to escape the world of external control he lives in just as Tom Sawyer and Huck Finn did more than a century ago. While Harry Potter is a phenomenon, there are many more high interest books that children could be introduced to in school. We cannot depend on text books to teach children the joy of reading. In a CBC, teachers may use text books but they don't count on children reading them for fun.

For example, the most common complaint about our schools is that not enough children are learning to read and currently a huge effort is being made to teach more of them to read better. But in my experience, we do teach the vast majority of our students to read. Our real failure is we don't introduce most of them, especially disadvantaged students, to the joy of reading. While reading is a valuable life skill, like all skills you have to use it or risk losing it.

Right now, at both the elementary and secondary levels, students who refuse to memorize information that both they and their teachers know they will soon forget, will be punished by low grades and failure. This is time they could spend reading, looking up information in books and using what they have looked up. Punishment for not memorizing is a destructive educational practice and possibly the clearest example of external control in the schools.

My son was forced to memorize the presidents in the order of their election to pass a high school history final. He did it but he hated his history teacher for making him do it and, for a long time afterwards, he hated history. But at least he did it.

How about the students who won't do it? They not only hate the teacher and hate history, they won't even try to learn it. This means that, if they won't do a lot of worthless memorizing, they won't graduate—hardly what anyone would call a desirable educational outcome. When students who come from disadvantaged homes do memorize and succeed, they do it far more because they like their teachers than because they see the usefulness of what they are asked to do. It is a shame that many good teachers waste their hard-earned goodwill with these students by asking them to expend it on a useless effort.

Most students who accept schooling do so because they come from affluent or educated families where the parents "schooled" and succeeded. More than any other practice it is this present emphasis on schooling that has led to the huge and growing disparity between the achievement of students from wealthy and/or educated families and the much lower achievement of students from less advantaged homes.

It is schooling that kills the excitement and joy in most academic classes. Both advantaged and disadvantaged students complain their classes are boring, but, like my son, most advantaged students do the work. They have enough going for them in their lives outside of school that they put up with schooling in class.

If you don't believe this, ask your own children how much of their assigned academic classwork and homework is exciting or joyful. Even as you ask that question, the incredulous look you'll see on their faces will answer it better than anything they may say. Ask them to forget about excitement and joy and tell you some things they are now learning that they see as useful to them in their lives, now or later, and you will see even more incredulity in their eyes.

The CBC has the potential to provide joy and excitement for all students and give the disadvantaged a much better chance to achieve. If we continue to school at the level we do now, one group will succeed but neither group will do much better than they do now. There is nothing motivating about learning without joy.

I am looking for teachers who want to be a part of the joy and excitement that comes with implementing Competence Based Classrooms. I believe the joy and success inherent in a CBC is crucial to achieving a well-educated, caring, and safe society. Our prisons are filled to bursting with school failures, most of whom come from poor families and who failed because schooling turned them off. Almost all of these men are capable. The schools failed them as much as they failed themselves.

The real world asks for competence and usually gets it when what they ask the worker to do is useful and they treat the worker well.

In the real world there is rarely any credit given for incompetence. Whenever you are asked to do anything at work, at home or anywhere else, competence is the minimum expected and accepted. Also, there is nothing about competence that is difficult to understand. The obvious reason the real world expects competence is to get a useful task done properly.

But there is a further important reason. If we are asked to do something we believe is useful by people who care about us *and we do it well*, both the askers and the doers feel good. The relationship between them is strengthened and the result is not only more competent work, but competent workers who will make an effort on their own to improve what they do towards quality.

Therefore, the bargain that successful managers or teachers in the real world make with anyone they ask to do anything is: *What I am asking you to do is useful. If you do not see its usefulness, I am more than willing to explain it to you. I accept you may not like to do what I'm asking, because it may be boring, difficult, strenuous or pay poorly. But you'll always know there is a good reason for me asking you to do it.*

In order to make the work more palatable (because a lot of work is not inherently pleasant), effective managers care about how their workers feel. If this care is evident, the workers will work hard even if the work, itself, is unpleasant. Caring management pays off because *the quality of work is directly proportional to how well workers get along with their manager.* This axiom applies as much to schoolwork as to the world of work outside of school.

Schoolwork (not schooling) may be useful, but its usefulness is rarely explained to students.

Unlike the real world, where the usefulness of the work is either obvious or explained, the usefulness of much of the work students are asked to do in their academic classes is neither obvious nor explained. The reason for most incompetent schoolwork is based on the often heard student complaint: *When'll I ever use this stuff?*

The less affluent the student, the less obvious the usefulness of knowledge much valued in our affluent culture, such as studying Shakespeare. Many students from disadvantaged homes, have little appreciation of our culture; they hardly know Public Television exists. The only place they can be exposed to culture, their school, often turns them off by asking them to memorize a lot of facts, as if painful memorization is the road to appreciating our cultural heritage.

I taught *Romeo and Juliet* to a high school class by asking the question, "What do you do when your parents don't like your girlfriend or boyfriend?"

They didn't need to memorize anything to get involved in that question and were amazed that parents 500 years ago were even worse than theirs. Usefulness does not depend on facts. It depends on your students seeing the connection between their life and what you are teaching. Whether you like it or not, you are the only one who can help them make that connection.

Title One, an enormous, well-intentioned program aimed at helping disadvantaged students succeed accomplished very little. Recent research on this expensive effort showed that for the 130 billion dollars spent in the last thirty years, there was no gain in student performance. The students were treated better but the schooling that blocked these children's ability to see the usefulness of what they were taught continued unchanged. The key to persuading students to make a greater effort to learn is taking the time to teach them the value of doing the work. With more teacher aides, the classroom climate in Title One classes improved but not enough to offset the destructiveness of *schooling*.

The school world, unlike the real world, does not ask for competence.

The school world is vastly different from the real world. It doesn't even come close to asking for competence. Few students who get below a B do competent work and no one knows this more than the students themselves. The working motto of underachieving students when questioned about their work is, "It's good enough." If school is supposed to prepare students for the real world, the present system of giving credit for "good enough" is not doing the job.

In the vast majority of schools today, the *stated goal* for teachers is to teach students enough so they do well on the state achievement tests. But to do well on these tests the students need to achieve higher than C and D grades in class. So in practice, unlike the stated goal, the *actual goal* is to teach students to do enough passing work to graduate. Graduation, not competence, is hailed by most school systems as an adequate measure of student accomplishment even if they do not do well on achievement tests.

In California, as reported in the *Los Angeles Times* (6/8/99), in an article headlined, "State's Graduation Rate Is Among Lowest in U.S.," the schools, even though they are giving low grades, are failing to keep students in school. Yet, there is nothing in that article that recommends schools give up low grades or require competence in a much more caring work place. The article offered no solution for this problem except to infer that the teachers are at fault, the standards need to be raised and more external control is needed.

Unlike the real world where managers are strongly encouraged to provide a satisfying work place so more workers will do competent work, secondary school teachers, especially in disadvantaged schools, are not strongly encouraged to provide a satisfying classroom environment beyond what it takes to get students to pass.

This is one reason why state test scores are improving at a much slower rate in the secondary schools than in the elementary schools where the teachers are now encouraged to provide a satisfying classroom environment. Ask your own children where they enjoyed schoolwork, in the elementary schools or secondary schools, and most will mention the early grades. Joy in school is not a "pie in the sky" idea, it is even more vital for school success at the upper grades than at the lower grades. That many high school teachers make an effort to provide such an environment is to their credit. But the system in which they work rarely recognizes them for this effort.

High school teachers who are unfriendly and uncaring are accepted, even esteemed, in many schools if the majority of their students do enough work to get credit. The attitude, "It's the student's problem, not the teacher's, if they don't want to learn," is all too common in secondary schools. Trapped in this incompetence-accepting, and often uncaring work place, most students become apathetic in their academic classes as they move up the school ladder. A few rebel and are labeled discipline problems, but it's amazing so few do. If workers in a business were treated as are so many secondary students in academic classes, by inferring that, *It's okay if you're incompetent, just show up and do a little work*, that business would soon go broke.

With the exception of the Johnson City, New York, School District under the leadership of Superintendent Albert Mamary as it operated in the years between 1976 to 1993, no other school district I know of has ever seriously suggested eliminating low grades and making competence (B grades) the minimal standard for credit. During those years, Johnson City schools were lauded nationwide. At the risk of repeating myself, I can't but wonder how we can demand better performance on state achievement tests and still give credit for low grades. All the present talk about accountability is meaningless because there is nothing to be accountable for in any school system that awards credit for incompetence.

Extracurricular activities are almost all competence based.

The one place in our schools where competence is almost always required of students who participate (a requirement usually well accepted by the involved students), is in the extracurricular activities such as athletics, music, drama, drill team and cheerleading. It is also required in the writing, editing and photography for the school newspaper and yearbook. Students who are not willing to strive for competence and beyond, seldom go out for these activities and, if they do, don't stick around very long. There are, however, no shortages of students who want to participate because there is joy, excitement and a lot of success in these useful pursuits. Students and teachers connect with each other in extracurricular experiences.

There may be a few teachers or coaches leading these activities who treat participants badly, but traditionally, the extracurricular climate is one of hard work in which teachers and students care for each other. Grades are not needed to motivate these participants. They are well aware that what they choose to do is worth doing because they understand its value and because it feels so good. Extracurricular activities are both popular and successful in the eyes of students, staff, parents, and the community. It's a shame we don't learn enough from their success to do the same in the classroom. In Ireland they are doing this.

The Transition Year, a competence based program new to Ireland, has been embraced with an enthusiasm not often seen in academic classes.

The Transition Year, the creation of a progressive Irish Department of Education and Science became an educational reality in 1994.[3] It is not only supported by the Department of Education but they actively proposed it and continue to encourage it. This is an extra year that students who have completed their Junior Certificate at age fifteen can elect instead of leaving school or moving on to the Senior Cycle.

What this year offers both students and teachers is a chance to work together to plan a program for a year. Typical content of this year includes work experience, information technology, personal and social development, the arts, technical studies, teaching and tutoring practice, communication skills, European awareness, modern languages and media education.

From an educational and motivational standpoint, the results have been outstanding. The excitement generated by this essentially competence based approach spread through the whole school positively affecting both teachers and students. Involved students, many of whom by age fifteen were ready to leave, now come to school early and stay late all through the year. Given a chance to get a little control over their own education, they show appreciation by working hard for themselves not just to satisfy school mandated requirements. They learn more about themselves than ever before and say, "This is the best year I've had in school."

According to Brian Lennon, a senior instructor for the William Glasser Institute, Ireland, and an educator in an Irish Secondary School, "The Transition Year has offered our teachers and students the freedom to focus on real learning. What emerges is a quality experience with a stronger sense of relevance in the curriculum, greater personal responsibility in the students, real pride in learning and a much more collaborative relationship between teachers and students."

"An example of one such programme chosen by our students is as follows: they invited a lecturer from a teacher training college to come and train them how to teach small children. They then apply these skills as Teacher Assistants in a neighboring primary school. The transition year in our school has helped students rediscover the joy of learning and, it must be added, has helped teachers find the joy of teaching."

In Brian's School, Saint Oliver's, students are given certificates for the different components of the transition year they complete successfully. Towards the end of the year, there is a special evening for them to show off their work to parents and friends.

Even though what goes on is so different from the usual way to learn, there has been no organized criticism or opposition to this innovative approach. The program is an unqualified success.

Further details on this program are available on the Saint Oliver's Web-site (www.socc.ie).

Art, music and vocational classes are competence based.

In voluntary classes like art and music, students may be graded, but they almost always make an effort and, if graded, the grade assigned is rarely less than a B, often an A. In the vocational courses, which are all taught with real world standards, there is little problem getting students to accept these obvious standards and competence is an absolute requirement for credit. In these classes, the students see the usefulness of what they are learning and, with an enthusiastic teacher there is a lot of joy in the class. The students may do some memorizing in the vocational classes but, when they do, they see the value because they use it every day to get the job done.

Pressuring low-income students to work is generally counterproductive.

There is some evidence that students from higher income and more educated families may work for credit if they are pressured, but competence is not increased by pressure regardless of family income. Pressuring students who have no family incentive to learn is not only useless, it is counterproductive. These students will expend what energy they have resisting the pressure, leaving little or no energy for doing what they most need to do: increase their efforts toward competence.

Except for real math, most students have some idea which educational skills are useful in the real world and which are not.

I have over forty years of experience in talking with students in private and public schools, and the five skills they all tell me they believe are useful in the real world are *reading, writing, calculating (which is not real math), science and using a computer.* When we talk, students actually say *math*, not calculation. But when asked to describe what math is, they describe calculation. My definition of real math is solving story problems be it figuring out how to get correct change in a store or solving problems in quantum physics. There is also such a thing as pure math but for me to attempt to define it is not appropriate in this book and has little to do with what goes on in pre-college math classes.

Even though many of the students I have talked with have passed some real math courses such as algebra and geometry or higher, they rarely mention these courses because most of them didn't feel competent even if they got a good grade. They mentioned that calculation, by hand or calculator, is useful in solving the simple math problems like figuring out batting averages. For all practical purposes it is the only math that most people know and use. We have a long way to go before many students mention higher math as useful to them in the real world, or before many students will be enthusiastic learners of higher math in school. But we ought to begin moving in this direction in all schools.

Huge numbers of students, especially if they come from advantaged homes, earn credit in math courses such as algebra, even when both they and the teacher know they have little ability to solve story problems such as when or where the trains meet by using algebra. Also few of them understand why it is important to learn higher math. Students seldom see anyone in the real world doing higher math. For most of them, it is a hurdle to jump over so, like you and me, they jump. For those who won't or can't jump, the way we now teach math in secondary schools is a nightmare. What it is or why they need it—except to get into college—starts and finishes as a mystery for almost all students except for those who are talented in this area.

The majority of students who come to school like the concept of *science* and think it worth learning. But unfortunately, most of what they do before high school chemistry and physics is memorize soon-to-be-forgotten science facts from a text. Few of them are taught what science actually is or how it is useful in the real world.

But from films such as *Star Wars*, television shows like *Star Trek*, and now the *Harry Potter* books, they get an inkling of what science might be. Unfortunately, these shows and books do not begin to explain real science or anything close to it. While science in the real world has nothing to do with *schooling*, it would be hard to figure this out by looking at the way it is taught and how it is evaluated in most elementary and middle schools.

Students tend to see *reading* as useful but, as I've already explained, little emphasis is put on providing interesting material to read. Middle schools and high schools are filled with students who know how to read but have never read a book for pleasure and have told me they never intend to. When I talk about reading for pleasure (pre Harry Potter) they look at me as if questioning my sanity.

Most students also see *writing* as useful, but the way much of it is taught, focusing on grammar they don't understand, results in reduced creativity, low grades and failure. Less than half the students learn to write competently in school, even though the ability to write competently correlates more highly with success on state achievement tests than anything else we teach except non-technical problem solving.

All students believe that *computer* skills are worth learning and many are skilled computer users. These students find computer skills so useful they do not depend on school to teach them to use one. But for those who do not have access to a computer or have no one outside of school to teach them to use one, schools should provide this education and right now most schools are attempting to do this. Learning computer skills is a very bright spot in our present schools even in many disadvantaged neighborhoods.

Unfortunately, few students believe that *history or social studies* is useful. These potentially fascinating subjects are more involved with *schooling*, i.e., memorizing historical facts that will soon be forgotten, than anything else taught in school. Although some teachers make these subjects come alive, the CBC will do a great deal to help these subjects become more compelling by eliminating schooling from the way they are taught. The saddest omission of our present schools is that two of the most important real world skills, *speaking and listening*, are never mentioned by students as useful because neither schools nor parents stress their importance. To get ahead in the real world, socially or economically, these skills are necessary. The only way to learn to speak and listen competently is to do it. Since there is seldom academic emphasis on practicing these skills, it is up to individual teachers to recognize their importance and engage students in a lot of practice. Some teachers do and some don't.

Learning the usefulness of real math, science and social studies is a priority in a CBC. Achieving competence in these subjects as well as in reading, writing, math and using a computer is also a high priority in a CBC. In learning these subjects in a CBC there would also be so much teacher-student or team interaction that speaking and listening skills would become a natural part of the curriculum.

Assessment: testing and grading

The authentic purpose of assessment, now called Formative Assessment when it achieves this purpose, is to help students to learn well. Low grades given before students are competent discourages them. In a CBC, grades would not be assigned until the teacher felt the students were competent and had reached the B level. After that, higher grades than a B could be achieved by doing more in-depth work. In the next chapter, I'll go into more detail on how this is done in a CBC.

With one important exception, memorization, teachers and parents generally agree with students on what is worth learning in school.

Both parents and teachers agree with students that *reading, writing, calculation (math), science and computer literacy* are useful. But, to these five, they add the skill of *memorizing*, perhaps the most educationally destructive aspect of schooling and a generally useless life skill. Actually the memorization they support so strongly is only short term: just remember it for the test. No one really expects students to retain all they temporarily memorize.

For parents and teachers, short-term memorization is the surest road to college and, except in the technical fields, is very important for educational success in college through the doctoral level. For students, memorization is almost never on the list of useful skills. Many capable students dislike school because of it. Temporary knowledge is valuable only in school; using knowledge is valuable everywhere, now and later.

The skills required for success in the work place.

Of the five skills useful to students (or six to teachers and parents if we add memorization), only three are widely valued in the work place: *reading, writing and computer literacy*. The real world never asks anyone to *memorize* anything that is not used daily or that can be easily and accurately looked up. At work, all *calculations are* done with calculators, and mistakes are not tolerated. Math and science, beyond simple problem solving, are left to college-trained experts or specifically taught if these skills are needed. Amateurs do not do higher math or science in the real world.

The six additional work place skills, *problem solving, applying knowledge, leading, cooperating, speaking and listening,* are neither required nor stressed in most classrooms. In a CBC, problem solving and applying knowledge would be a major part of all that is taught. This should be the real purpose of spending time learning history, social studies and literature. In these subjects, it's not just who did it or what happened that counts, but why he or she did it, how he or she could have done it better, and what could be learned from the experience. Doing this would be good practice for what is demanded above all else in the real world work place: *non-technical problem solving based on applying or using knowledge.*

Beyond these skills, success in the real world, depends on how well the workers and managers get along together, so many companies make a significant effort and spend a lot of money teaching *cooperation and leadership.* But in order to cooperate and lead, *they need to speak and listen* in ways that help the people at work connect with each other. Unfortunately, these skills can only be learned through practice and example. Here the real world and school world both come up short: neither allots enough time for practicing communication and connecting skills.

I can see why work doesn't do this; not enough time. But there is no excuse for not doing it in school where it can be a part of nearly every academic class.

To depend on people to learn to speak and listen effectively mostly on their own, as we do now, makes no sense. In a CBC these skills would be practiced daily as part of the regular teaching effort. This is the surest way to learn them.

In an ideal world, to get credit, all students would have to be competent.

Based on the false belief that large numbers of students are unable to do competent work, most schools are not ready to raise their standards to the competence-for-credit level that the CBC requires. But in the chapters that follow, I contend that, if we can get rid of external control, we can convince almost every student to work hard enough for the CBC to work well in any class. Giving an incomplete to students who don't do enough to get credit gives them a chance to learn. A low grade or failure shuts them down.

Our experience from the Glasser Quality Schools confirms this contention. Credit is withheld for incompetence but there are almost no incompetent students. Incompetence becomes a non-problem. When we offer students a chance for competence in a way they believe they can actually become competent, they overwhelmingly accept the offer. In fact, judging by their state achievement test scores, many students in a GQS are not willing to settle for competence. They want to go further and do superior work.

Because when we couple the strong teacher-student relationships with eliminating schooling it is actually more enjoyable to do competent work than to slide along incompetently as so many students do now. The problem with requiring competence is not in the students' heads, it's in the heads of administrators, teachers and parents who believe that most students, especially disadvantaged ones, have to be forced to learn. They believe it because this is the way it's been for centuries. But it's not the way it has to be and it's not the way it is in a GQS.

When I hear prominent citizens such as politicians, business leaders and even school leaders talk about improving education, they always speak in very general terms as if what goes on in the classroom is okay. All we have to do is do it harder. They almost never mention *problem solving, using knowledge or speaking and listening*, all very important skills in the real world, no matter what task is attempted. It is rare to hear anyone in a position of power talk seriously about how important it is for schools to provide a caring environment. Mostly what they talk about is using more external control.

Competence is the core of all success and most happiness, no matter what we choose to do with our lives. Competence should be the core value of our schools. In the work place where competence is the core value, incompetent workers are eventually discharged or not promoted. But in school, students are neither discharged for incompetence nor should they be. We need to make a serious effort to help them achieve competence instead of what we are doing now including social promotion. To our credit, there is a strong movement away from social promotion. What I am trying to start is an even stronger movement toward success for all students.

Seven

A New Way To Teach

The way most teachers teach now has not changed in a hundred years: teach, then test, then grade, teach some more, test again and repeat the *teaching testing grading* until the year is over. Both the teaching and the learning almost always end with the test. In the ABCDF grading system, each test is graded and the largest part of the final grade is an average of the test grades. Grades on assignments, class discussion and homework also play a part but, most of the teaching and learning end when the tests are graded. The records show the grades on these other activities will be similar to the grades on the tests and neither tests nor assignments will be improved after they are graded. A student who does well on the tests will generally do well on other work and vice versa.

The variables in the process are the *teaching*, the *tests*, the *assignments*, and the *motivation* of the students. When the *teaching is good*, the *tests fair*, the *assignments interesting* and the students *highly motivated* this system produces excellent results. If we improve the teaching, the results will be better but there is no more chance to improve the teaching significantly than there is to noticeably improve any other profession that works with people. There are good and bad teachers, doctors, lawyers and other professionals and no way in our present system to make them better. In-service training doesn't begin to do the job.

As long as we train the teachers in the *teach and then test method* and use the ABCDF grading system, there is no reason to expect that, in the foreseeable future, teaching will get better or worse. It will stay the way it is.

Can we improve the tests or the assignments the teachers use in their classrooms? This is also unlikely since the same teachers construct the tests and figure out the assignments. There are no standard tests or standard assignments that teachers use in their classrooms. And please be clear, I am not suggesting there should be.

The last variable is student motivation and we have extremely accurate long-term information on that. As stated previously, the results on mass achievement tests such as the SAT and various state achievement tests are directly correlated with family income. The richer the family, the better the results. There is also a high relationship between good results and the level of education in the homes but, of course, an education-supporting home environment and high family income are directly related. As long as we use the present system, don't expect any change in student motivation.

Recent research[4] shows that disadvantaged elementary school students, not secondary students, are more motivated and do better on achievement tests if they are in smaller classes, had preschool and access to richer educational material. But here again we are looking at the effect of more money. Whether we can motivate disadvantaged secondary students (who are much more aware of their poverty than elementary students) by spending more money on their education has not yet been shown.

The recent increases in student achievement in California were restricted to the lower grades of the elementary schools. More money may pay off in secondary schools but there are many more motivation killing disadvantages to being poor than going to inadequately funded high schools.

It is also obvious that in the foreseeable future we may never close the now widening gap between the rich and the poor. There will be more funding for rich schools than poor schools especially at the secondary level. This means that, even with increased state aid to the elementary schools, we may not be able to do anything more than we are doing now to improve the secondary schools.

These are the present facts of life. I, for one, am not willing to accept these facts. I have seen what can be done in GQS's and I think it could be done in any school, even high schools, if we would give the CBC a chance. It doesn't cost anymore than we are spending now, it doesn't require different teachers and it doesn't do away with tests, assignments or grades. And in the present GQS's it has led to significantly higher test scores. If what has been achieved at Aikman were continued on through graduation, I have no doubt those students would be at the top of all students in Texas.

But as I will now describe it, the CBC is a significant change in the present system of teaching, testing, grading—a change that is simple and clear. You teach and then test; that much is the same. But after you test, you keep teaching until all the students who took the test have answered all questions competently or correctly. By making only this small change in the traditional system, we can mobilize a huge source of student and teacher motivation that is rarely tapped now.

Think of all the tests you have taken and how many times you walked out of a test and said to yourself, 'If I could've had a little more time I could've really nailed that exam. Or, oh, now I see the correct answer but it's too late. Or, I just couldn't put what was in my mind on a sheet of paper. But if I'd had a chance to talk about that question with the teacher I could have explained what I was thinking about. Or, that question wasn't clear; I didn't know how to answer it. If I had a chance, I'd have asked the teacher to explain it. Or, all the things I studied for weren't on the test. It isn't fair. Why couldn't I have a chance to tell the teacher what I know? I think what I've learned is more important than what was asked on the test.' I'm sure there's ten other things that I can't think of but which may have crossed your mind on many occasions.

Have you ever finished a course and said to yourself, 'I could have done a lot better but all the other students in the class were so much smarter than me. Every time I opened my mouth I felt like a fool. Finally I just gave up. Or, it's not fair to grade on a curve. I got over ninety on every test but I only got a B. I deserved an A. Or, the only difference between me and an A student is they memorize a lot of stuff that most of us forget. If that teacher thinks memorizing is so important why doesn't he go teach elephants? Or, I know that some of the kids who got them all right, cheated. I saw them. Why don't they give tests that no one can cheat on?' Or a lot more gripes about what went on in school that could've been done better or with more fairness.

If these thoughts still come to your mind as they come to mine, you should seriously consider the CBC. I'll explain it as if you'd be starting it in the fall with a new class or classes. In actual practice you can start it any time in the first semester. It might be started in the second semester but more as a trial to see if your students liked it. There wouldn't be enough time for a full fledged experiment. Anyway, as with all I suggest in this book, you can be the judge.

The success of the CBC depends on whether you can convince the students that it's worth working for competence. Tell them honestly that you don't think it's fair to give them credit for less than competent work. But then say, "I have a new way to teach called the Competence Based Classroom in which everyone in this room can do competent or B work." When you say that they'll be skeptical. They've heard a lot things like that before, especially your telling them it's not fair to give them credit for not doing much work. But don't worry if they're skeptical, at least they are interested and more likely to listen to the rest of what you're going to say.

Immediately, a student who is used to external control will ask, "What happens if I don't do B work?...You gonna flunk me?"

You can answer, "The only way you won't do it is if you don't try. When I explain to you what you have to do, I think you'll try. If you still don't want to do the work, we'll talk it over and figure out what to do then. But no one's going to flunk. Before any of you make up your minds, let's give it a try. If no one wants to do it then we'll go back to the old way: low grades and failure for a lot of students; good grades and success for less than half of you."

I suggest you try the CBC and let you and your students be the judge. If it works as it usually does when you do what I'm going to explain in this chapter, you may still have a few problems. But there is more information in this book that will help you handle most of the problems that might arise. Don't worry about that now. You may not have any problems.

In this chapter, I'll explain in general terms what a CBC is. In chapters eight and nine that follow, I'll explain in very specific terms what you actually do when you start the year if you are an elementary or secondary school teacher. Since, this is a new way for you to teach, the more you understand before you start explaining it to your class, the better chance you'll have to get off to a good start.

First, some common elements in the CBC that apply both to elementary and secondary schools.

I think the most difficult part of moving to the CBC at any level is accepting the idea that, essentially, all students are capable of competent work. If you can accept that, you're still going to have an almost equally hard job convincing all your students that they are capable. The earlier you start the CBC, the better, because by the end of the first grade, some students have already made up their minds about how much they are capable of doing in school. If it's not very much they may already see themselves as seven-year-old failures. This happens now in the present ABCDF system because not only do teachers rank the students, the students rank each other. The A and B students are used to getting most of your attention; they won't want to share you with the students who have never done much work. When you start the CBC and begin to give the low performers attention, the good students may resent it. But when they find out they can still get A's with no schooling, they'll get over their resentment.

The C and D students have a different problem, they'll worry that you're going to force them to do more work than they have ever done, more than many of them think they are capable of doing. If you work in schools where students are tracked, both you and the low track students will have the same worries. Yours will be, 'Can I actually teach them all to do competent work?' Theirs will be, 'Am I actually capable of doing competent work?' In the rest of this chapter, I'll use my words to explain what I suggest you do. Feel free to interpret my explanation in words your students understand. Don't feel you have to use my language.

What you will do as you begin in the fall with the first unit of work is about the same as you do now. Explain clearly what you are going to teach them and what they have to do to be competent. It doesn't matter whether they are in elementary or high school, your job is to explain the immediate task ahead. You might also give them a very general idea of where they will be by the end of the year but tell them the only thing they have to be concerned about right now is the first unit you're just about to explain. You may also tell them that each unit will not be that much different from what they're now going to start. You don't have to change the way you actually instruct. Just be sure to explain how and where what you teach can be useful to them.

Then you'll begin to explain what is new in a CBC: All the students will be asked to learn whatever the unit calls for to the level of competence and they'll get a B grade for learning it. What you're going to do is make a B or competence the lowest grade you'll give. If it weren't asked before, this is where a student will ask, 'What happens if I don't do the work?' Don't worry, just tell them to be patient and trust you.

You'll then explain that to get a B they will all pass tests at the level of competence, and other assignments at that level, too. But here, only talk about the tests. The way you deal with everything else will be the same. Tell them there'll be a lot of tests, and at some points in the year there may be two or three tests a week. Students who haven't done competent work in the past will become alarmed, even the good students will be skeptical. As in Star Trek, you are going places few teachers have been before.

But you will deal with their alarm by saying, 'Don't worry about it, let's try it and see what happens.' You will then teach a small amount of the first unit the way you would ordinarily teach it. Then after you have taught the unit, tell them, now you'll have a test on it. Remind them that as you taught, you went over some possible test questions and alerted them these could be on the test. If they asked if something else would be on the test, tell them anything you covered might be on the test as well as anything in the book. Tell them to study the book and their notes and they'll be fine. They are free to use their books and notes.

As you presented your material or discussed it with them, you should point out that none of the questions you're going to ask them will require they memorize anything. You want them to get the ideas and to be able to demonstrate their ability to understand and use what you've taught. You might give them a short, one-question, practice test a few days ahead of time and go over their answers in class so they get the idea of what is expected. What you'll be asking are thinking questions like a story problem in math or a question about the point of an essay in their English text.

As you teach the first unit, you will emphasize the

difference between acquiring knowledge and using it as well as improving it. You will have explained schooling and told them you don't teach or test that way. You will also have encouraged discussion as you've gone through the first part of the unit. If they are very small children, you'll point out what you have been talking about is thinking. The test may require they talk to you and they can't talk without thinking. Writing will come later when they have learned how but add, you can't write without thinking either.

You will also weave the idea of competence and competent ideas into your presentation and use some examples to show them the difference between competent and incompetent thinking. Give them a chance to discuss what is competent and what is not. Tell them when they study to try to focus on understanding and using ideas. Ask them to share with their parent or parents what they have been learning and share with them what they are studying for the test. Tell them to ask their parents if they have any suggestions on what is important to study. The first test is a big deal. Talk a lot about it and don't be in a rush. If it takes a few weeks to get that far, it's okay. Continue to assure them not to worry. They'll all be competent.

Right before they start taking the test tell them again because they may not believe you want them to use any book, their notes and any other material they want. Tell them they can ask other students for help but the students don't have to help. That's up to each of them. But also tell them if they get stuck they can ask you. But if they do that, they'll have to wait their turn and that could take up a lot of time.

If you see a lot of them having trouble with a question, you might stop right in the middle of the test and teach them what they need to know that will help them over the part they were stuck on. This is a perfect teaching moment. You'll have their undivided attention. Tell them you enjoy helping them on the test because it is important to you that they answer the questions competently. Again, you are sending the message that you're their friend, not their adversary.

About half way through the test again remind them to work hard because you are going to read their test with them and talk it over. The better they do, the more you'll both enjoy talking about the test. Together, you and they will work out their grade and what to do if they are not yet competent. Tell them that when you and they get together, you may ask them to explain to you why they wrote what they did. Tell them they don't have to worry about time. If they aren't finished, they can take the test home and finish it there. They can get help at home if it is available or work on it with a friend from the class if they want to. But as soon as they finish, they should let you know and you'll go over their test personally with them.

As you go over what they wrote, you'll talk to them about their answers and, if some aren't complete or competent, they'll have a chance to go back to their seat and work some more. You can explain that you will be the judge of whether what they wrote was competent. But to get credit they will also have to explain to you why they wrote what they did so you know that it wasn't a guess, or something they copied but didn't understand. You want to know that they knew what they were doing.

Since this will take some time, it would be wise to restrict the first tests to only a few questions so you would have time to do this properly. One or two good questions you can talk to them about for a minute or two will usually give you an accurate idea of what they know. It is okay for the other students in the class to listen in when you talk to each student. They may learn something they need to know. This isn't a competition: the goal is competence for everyone.

For most students this will be the first time this has ever happened. On previous tests they would get a grade and that was it. There would be no incentive to work further on the questions they missed or to explain why they wrote what they did. This is different. You aren't interested in marking what they got wrong. You are very interested in helping them correct their mistakes and do a good job. If they need help, there is plenty available.

Since there would be no memory questions which now clog up tests, one or two essay questions and/or four or five multiple-choice questions would be enough. On the multiple-choice questions, they would be asked to do more than come up with the correct choice; they would explain why it's correct. If they got it wrong they would keep trying until it is right and can explain why. On multiple-choice they would always have the option of suggesting a better answer to the question along with the reason why it is better. If it makes sense, you would accept, even encourage, this out-of-the-box thinking.

Since this first test would occur at the beginning of the year it would pay to take a lot of time to walk the whole class through this experience. The first tests are the prototype for the rest of the year. This is the time to work the bugs out of the new system.

If a student did well on his first attempt at the test, and you knew from class discussions that he was competent, you wouldn't need more than a moment or two to go over his test. Of course, if he wanted a little more of your time, you would give it to him. If you are mostly working with what have been good students, many of them would quickly do quite well in this new system. This will give you time to deal with the others. Evaluating a test should not be so time-consuming that you can't give personal attention when needed.

Let's say that with thirty in the class, ten were obviously competent shortly after they handed in their test. The rest would need to do more work and would need time with you as they moved toward competence. The idea is for you to be very patient at first as they were getting used to this new way to learn. Don't be in a hurry since it is this post-test work, seldom done in the present system, that gives the CBC its strength. You are tapping into motivation that in the present system goes untapped.

It is this working after the test when they have the actual questions in front of them and, most importantly can get credit for answering them competently, that helps students to focus and buckle down. Now all the guesswork is removed. They can go to their books and really read them as they search for what they need to know to answer the questions they didn't answer competently. This will ratchet up reading ability among students who need this practice most. As they realize this is all for their benefit, they will not consider this post-test work a waste of time. It is effort that has an immediate payoff: a good grade and credit.

There would be two incentives for the students who complete the test quickly and competently to keep working. One would be to volunteer to become an apprentice teacher-assistant (TA) and tutor the students who need help to become competent on the test. If they tutored at least one student to competence on the test, they could raise their own grade on the same test from a B to an A.

In my experience, it is very effective for a competent student to tutor a less competent one as long as the student being tutored is serious in wanting to finish the test correctly. In this instance, the students being tutored would have this motivation. The tutoring is worth an A to the tutor because there is no better way to learn than to teach and the tutors would learn a lot more. As the year went on, you would move the students who were effective tutors from apprentice to full TA status.

The other incentive for competent students would be to answer another, even more probing, question on the same test that, if answered competently, could raise their grade to an A. I believe there would always be students who preferred one option over the other. But a highly competent student would not have to choose. She could do both: tutor in the class and answer the extra question at home. Keep in mind there is no ceiling in a CBC, only a competent floor. This would be a way for a hardworking student to earn beyond an A to an A+.

While there would be no failure and several ways to get immediate help toward competence, you would stress that if a student got too far behind, he would have to take an incomplete and, to get credit, would have to do the work later on competently. This make up could be done at home, in the summer or the next year. If the student were too far behind, he would have to repeat the course. There would be no social promotion.

This is not external control; it is a choice. You would make it your business to point out the real world has time limits and so does the CBC. If it could be arranged, there would be no failure, no F's on their transcript only what you hope will be a temporary incomplete. Like in the real world, the transcript would record only courses finished with a B. To graduate, they would need the same number of credits needed now. The difference would be that the transcript would only reflect competence, whether the student graduated or not. That would be a huge improvement over the many meaningless transcripts filled with low grades and failure that comprise school records now.

This approach eliminates all the empty political talk of raising standards. This is really raising standards, but, at the same time, setting up a workable system to reach them. In a CBC you would never reduce the amount of work that has to be covered for competence. The only variable would be time. You could increase the time by Saturday classes, night classes or vacation classes. But don't worry that this would be an option many students would choose. My experience is once they believe you are serious about competence and allow them all the opportunities I've explained to show you competent work, the number of students who refuse to do the work in the time allotted would be insignificant.

By offering this extra time, you continue to send the message you are serious about competence. The students don't want to spend extra time in school any more than you do. Some schools do have the provision for Saturday detention. If they are willing to spend money on that ineffective external control punishment, I see no reason for them not to spend the money on serious, voluntary Saturday classes for students who need extra time to become competent. This is a message we don't come close to sending now with our ABCDF grading system.

At first, it would be important to adjust the difficulty of the tests starting with easy questions and then moving on to more challenging ones. For most of your students, competence is a very new idea and it'll take time for them to realize you are serious. The students would catch on to the standard of competence at different rates and you might have to personally tutor a small group of students who were having trouble adjusting even with more time and help. This would allow you to focus some of your attention on the students who needed you most. The ones who catch on will do their work and, if they need it, can get help from the tutors. This personal support would make it very difficult for any student to blame you for his not working.

I can't anticipate all the variations in this approach but once you catch on, with your skills, creativity and good judgement I believe you'll be able to handle the problems. Don't forget, under this system the students are not your adversaries. Once they catch on and trust you, they will want to earn a competent grade just as much as you want them to. But also remember not to underestimate the power of good relationships. There is no external control in the CBC. The relationships in the CBC are more like what is now achieved in the extracurricular activities than in the regular classrooms.

If there is a student whom you don't think has the ability to do competent work, you would talk with your principal and decide what to do. For these challenged students, there could be a lower level of work but you could still certify they were competent at this lower level.

When I worked at the Ventura School, we were surprised at how just eliminating failure was motivating enough to move most of them, many whose record questioned their ability to do competent schoolwork, to try hard and do it as long as we were patient and gave them enough time. The CBC has that time built into it at the beginning. A slow, careful start is the road to a fast competent finish.

As we go on to the next chapters covering the specifics of a CBC in the elementary school and secondary school, I'm confident that most questions you have at the end of this chapter will be answered.

Eight

The Competence Based Classroom
In an Elementary School

It helps that we already have four Glasser Quality Elementary school models that I encourage you to visit. Many others are working toward this goal but these have taken the final step: declaring what they have accomplished. This does not mean they have stopped improving. But it does mean that, essentially, all the students are competent learners and many are doing quality or A work. In these schools, students, teachers and many parents have learned enough choice theory to begin to put it to use in their lives. There may be occasional discipline incidents but almost never recurring discipline problems. Students may enter labeled ADD, ADHD or ODD but in less than a year, they are paying attention and need no special help. All these schools score very high on the state achievement tests.

The challenge for elementary school teachers is accepting that very young students mature at different rates. What may seem to be an inability to attend to school work or to concentrate in kindergarten and the primary grades may be due to different rates of brain maturation. At this age children are very sensitive to external control. They are in the process of moving from a world that revolved around them to a world now asking them to do things they may see no sense in doing.

Their ability to accept this change is related to how mature they are and there is no way of knowing precisely how mature that is so, if you err on the side of not expecting too much too soon, you will be safe. For example, you can tell one child to sit down and he sits down. You tell another child, who doesn't act much different from the first, to sit down and he pays no attention to what you said. How you treat this second child may have a lot to do with his school success from that time on.

Believe me, I know that when you are trying to manage twenty to thirty very young children it is extremely difficult to avoid using external control. And when I say, external control, I don't mean that you get punitive or harsh. But from working for many years in the classrooms of four elementary schools in Southeast Los Angeles, I learned how sensitive children are at that age to the expression on your face, the gestures you make with your hands and the tone of your voice. It is here that it pays to keep the choice theory admonition clearly in mind: Is my demeanor or the words I'm using now with this child going to disconnect me from him, or is it going to keep or increase the connection we already have?

If you sense that the child is withdrawing you might consider changing your demeanor. Relax. Be a little more gentle and a little more patient. Even though you are being pressured from all sides by people who want you to prepare them for college in kindergarten, try not to worry about a child who isn't interested in decoding words or adding up apples as fast as he or she is supposed to be. Focus on all the things little children need to know that have little or nothing to do with reading, counting or a stop sign. For example, can they follow directions from you that are simple and sensible and are not the prelude to an academic task?

By this, I mean that when you ask him to sit down, it is to help him get ready to do something he likes to do such as to eat the morning snack, get ready for recess, cluster around while you read to a group that includes him, get ready to play a game or sing a song: all activities a kindergartner is mature enough to do and enjoy. If he is not mature enough to do these, he will certainly not be mature enough to do early academics and will resist any attempt on your part to force him to get involved.

Keep in mind that kindergarten is the place where children of different maturity levels learn to make the social adjustment to a classroom they all need to make. All the pleasurable activities listed above are for gaining the social skills needed to function in a classroom. To actually become skilled in any of these activities themselves in unimportant.

One thing that has worked well in many schools I've been involved with, is ask someone to donate a big old upholstered chair or couch you can call the *easy* or *happy* chair or any other name you want to give it. Maybe the class can figure out a name. Tell them when any of them find that things are getting too hard for them or they're unhappy, they can go to the chair and relax.

The rules of the chair are simple. They don't have to do anything at all while they are sitting there except be quiet. Once they feel better they can go back to their regular seats. They can go on their own or you could suggest they need a rest.

Once in a while tell them, things are getting hard for me right now and I need a few minutes in the chair. I'm not going to do anything or say anything, I just need a little time to relax. Doing this will give them a model for the use of the chair. Also they will see that you, too, are human and it will help them to connect with you. If they are totally out of order and nothing I've suggested works, you'll have to discuss them with your principal. In a GQS, you are not expected to work miracles.

This maturation differential has been handled well at the first Quality School, Huntington Woods, in Wyoming, Michigan, by grouping students at two or three levels in double classes of fifty students with two teachers. Kindergarten students may be combined with first graders, first and second may be combined as well as third, fourth and fifth. Flexible, what-works, grouping guides the staff at this school and may be something to consider doing in your school if you have the physical ability to combine two classes.

This way there is no abrupt year-end mandatory movement. Given time they all catch on and they progress in the class by readiness rather than age. Huntington Woods is not a static place. To see what they are doing now, you'd have to visit. Even though there have been changes—quality never stands still— what they do, and why they do it, is well-described in the book, *Quality is the Key: Stories from Huntington Woods*, by Sally Ludwig and Kaye Mentley.

Like almost everything else you'd like to start in school, it is easier to implement the GQS idea in an elementary school than in a secondary school. First, it is a lot easier to create the good relationships needed if you have only twenty to thirty children all week long. Second, it is easier to stop giving low grades; if the children are happy and learning, most parents are satisfied and won't push to keep C's, D's and F's. Third, time is more flexible. Fourth, the children have had much less experience with external control, which is a huge advantage. Fifth, at this level skills like reading, writing and calculating are recognized as more important than acquiring a lot of knowledge. To these skills in a Glasser Quality Elementary School, they add speaking, listening and problem solving.

Besides these skills there is some important knowledge that needs to be memorized and retained in an elementary school. The students should learn to spell accurately, learn basic math facts like the times tables and some important facts of history, geography, science and health. There may be other fact areas but they would all be handled the way I suggest here. This does not contradict the *no schooling edict* of the last chapter because no student's grade or credit is based on memorized knowledge.

In order to memorize this necessary knowledge, students need a lot of enjoyable practice with no chance to get anything wrong. Facts needed for each grade should be made available to every child in a little booklet or its equivalent. You could make it up for the first graders and as they learned to read and write they could start entering these essential facts as they committed them to memory. How you make the facts readily available to the students is up to you. The booklet is only a suggestion.

Some of you might use charts on the wall. Spelling words might be pasted on or hung from the ceiling to supplement material in each child's possession. What is important is when the children are checked on a fact, *that fact should be easily available to every child*. This way, as they learn them, any mistake they make is easily and immediately correctable. As I said previously, we do not learn from making mistakes, we learn from correcting them.

When you make the facts available, try to make them available in context. For example the word, *elephant*, would be followed by *the largest animal that lives on land*. *George Washington* would be followed by *the father of our country* or *the first president*. The word, *moon*, would be followed by *circles the earth and controls the tides*. The spelling word, *principal*, would be followed by the name or picture of your school principal. The math fact, *6 x 6*, would be in a multiplication square of *one through ten* for the primary grades and *one through twenty* for the fourth and fifth grades. Taught this way they won't have any trouble learning the times tables up through twenty by the end of the fifth grade. Their parents will be impressed and very supportive of what you are doing.

I suggest that a short fact test should be given at least once a day or maybe more. The children will love the fact tests because they cannot make a permanent mistake. You could test for one subject like spelling or you could mix subjects up like ten spelling words followed by ten multiplication facts. The rule would be everyone has to get every fact right on every test but all they have to do to get them right is copy them from wherever they are located. Looking for them could even be a fun game. In this instance, competence is getting everything to be memorized completely correct, or corrected immediately if there is a mistake.

The familiarity of repetition and the assurance they can't make a permanent mistake would make these frequent tests a lot of fun. For little children doing the same thing over and over and succeeding is very enjoyable and this way of teaching makes the facts almost impossible not to be retained. Little children have good memories when memorization makes sense to them. To avoid mistakes, the rule would be to check each other's work and, whenever a mistake was found, both the person who made the mistake and the person who found it would write down the word or fact correctly in a booklet labeled, *Mistakes I Have Corrected or Helped To Correct.* This is just another suggestion. Do what works best for you.

The tests, for competence, would be thinking tests as described in the last chapter. If they were written, the rule at all grade levels would be all facts would have to be correct or corrected in order to get credit for competence. The children would be encouraged to take their fact books home and get their parents to test them on the facts the same way: always allowing them to use the book to correct mistakes.

The children could be encouraged to test their parents so their parents can see how much they have learned and to appreciate how hard it is to remember facts and information we hardly ever use. For example, the word chrysanthemum might stump most parents. Parents would be encouraged to teach the children new facts that they thought were important but it would be up to you as to whether you wanted to add the new fact to the ones they are required to learn at that grade level. Using short frequent tests would mean that only a small amount of time would be devoted to learning facts. This would also eliminate the homework children hate the most, memorizing by themselves at home.

After a while the teacher would challenge students to close their fact book or not look at the posted facts as the test was given in order for them to see how well they had mastered the material. They would still check their answers and correct all mistakes. This would give them a little more of a challenge but still, in the end, everyone would succeed. I urge you to think of a better system or a more creative way to use this system that is fun for you and your students. The only caution is make sure all errors are immediately corrected. That part is crucial to the success of what I'm suggesting.

At the elementary level, a lot of the teaching would be oral through class discussions. Or an alternative could be small group discussions led by you, an aide, a parent, an older student working as a TA in your class or by a very competent student while the others are working. You cannot give them too much or too many of these learning discussions. Through this process, the children would get practice in speaking and listening, perhaps the two most important life skills that we spend too little time on now.

All through elementary school, there should be a major focus on reading. This is so important, I'll devote a special chapter to it later. Here I just want to say, that as important as reading is, you should be very careful not to overdo it. And it can be overdone. I was struck by the following letter I read in the paper recently. It speaks eloquently for itself.

At my daughter's school, the principal has made reading a priority. There are read-a-thons, daily reading records, "1000 Days to Reading Success" (beginning with reading instruction in kindergarten), Christopher Nance's special reading program, the "Cool Cougar Reader" program and a reading competition where the class that reads the most books gets to throw water balloons at the principal. One-third of my daughter's class was pulled out of class each day for

special reading intervention at the expense of math,
social studies, music and physical education.
And yet compared with her school's 1999 (Stanford 9)
reading scores, the 2000 reading scores remained the
same or went down. However in math, which received
much less emphasis, the scores improved. There's a
lesson in there somewhere.
My daughter has learned to dislike reading already
and she still has at least eleven more years of school.
What a shame.

Reading is no different from anything else that is
forced on us for our own good by well meaning people.
We resist. There is no limit to the ability of external
control to harm or destroy all it touches. There is no
more powerful way to teach children to appreciate
reading, at any level up through high school, than to
read to the students from a book they all like. These
books are available; your job is to find them.

The worst thing you can do is make reading a competition because in all competitions there are losers. In
the CBC there are no losers. Some good students may
be disgruntled because poor students are now getting
B's. Good students who used to get A's, simply by
memorizing may also be unhappy. These are problems
which most teachers can learn to deal with. Making
sure you have a good relationship with these students
and pointing out they still have a chance to get A's by
thinking and working creatively will usually solve the
problem.

Competence based tests, both oral and written,
would gradually start and then increase as the students
moved toward middle school. Without repeating
myself, it would be up to you to adapt the ideas in the

last chapter to the age of your students. But the same standards would apply. All children would need to be competent for credit. TA's would be selected as early as the last part of the second grade from your own students and loving competent students from the higher grades could be occasionally recruited to be TA's for the lower grades. Parents and grandparents who have the time could be encouraged to help, especially to read to students and to tutor. But parents would never evaluate students for competence; that could lead to problems.

An interesting variation proven by research to be valuable is to use very bright young students to volunteer to read to, or tutor, older students who need help. Once the older students see how skilled the young TA's are, they get the idea if that little kid can do it, I can do it, too.

The thrust of the CBC at any level is to make competent learning so possible that all the students will refuse to settle for less. Instead of using their energy to resist learning, as many in our external control schools do now, they can use the same energy to work for competence and beyond. The idea again is to communicate in as many ways as you can that competence is the floor not the ceiling. The CBC can be a rising tide that raises all students.

Robert Sullo, in his book, *Inspiring Quality In Your School*, suggests, "As educators, let us remember that every human, regardless of their developmental or cognitive level, wants to learn how to be more skilled, more competent. We can see it in the newborn. It expresses itself in the preschooler on a regular basis. When we respect that universal human need in our classrooms, students discover healthy, responsible ways to increase their sense of power in the world.

They are less likely to be driven to get power "over" other people in destructive ways and more likely to become powerful beings who make valuable contributions to our world."

What the CBC does, because there are no losers, is stop the worrying that uses up so much student energy now. It is surprising that even very little children are worried about school success. They worry they'll forget something or they won't have another chance. With the CBC, as long as the student is willing to work, he or she never runs out of chances. It's sort of like betting on the horse after the race is over. You still have to make the effort to place the bet but you can't lose. Nothing is more discouraging than to study hard and then find that the test is on the one thing you missed. In real life you always know what the test is on. The winners in real life are the ones who make the effort, not the ones who depend on guessing games.

When you teach this way, you can be a true collaborator in the learning process. You send the message strongly, I want to help you to be competent or go beyond. We are in this class together. My job is to teach you and help you to learn; my job is not to find out what you don't know and punish you for not knowing it. If you have a question, ask me. If you need more time I'll give it to you. If you have an idea how to do what we're trying to do better, tell me. I'll listen.

The main thing to me is that as we learn we also have fun. We can work together to make school the place you want to be most. At Huntington Woods, the only complaint parents have had in recent years is that the children won't tell them when they are sick; they don't want to miss school. Some things in life are very hard. Learning in a CBC isn't one of them.

Nine

The Competence Based Classroom in the Secondary School

Creating a CBC is more difficult in a secondary school than in an elementary school for several obvious reasons: many more students, much more concern about eliminating C, D and F grades, and far less flexibility about time are three that come to mind. But even more than these specific reasons, there is much more tradition in the secondary school and the CBC is a break with most of what we have done for centuries. The CBC, however, is not a break with real world educational tradition. A law student can take the state bar as many times as he wants and will be given the same credit for passing as a student who passed it the first time.

Therefore, I suggest that only the secondary school teachers who read this book and want to try the CBC in their classroom teach the first CBC's in their school. Even then I suggest that only a few need pioneer this process and none be pressured to do it. The same should be true for the first students. They too, should be volunteers and not participate without their parents' permission. Even then, if the CBC is started in the fall when school begins, I suggest any student who wants to could withdraw from the CBC after five weeks and be transferred to a regular class. If it works as well as our experience shows it will, there will be plenty of students who will volunteer to replace the students who have withdrawn.

However, no teacher need wait for the beginning of the year to start a CBC. An interested teacher could talk to her students any time during the school year and ask them if they'd like to try one unit, perhaps for two weeks, the CBC way. The CBC would lend itself well to a short trial. There would be no need to get parental permission. If it worked, it is from the word of these students and their friends that whole classes could be recruited to start the next school year.

The best way to evaluate something new is to try it in actual practice. If it works, its value will be obvious. If enough teachers try it, there will be sufficient success so that teachers who did not succeed could get together with teachers who succeeded and try to figure out what went wrong. You wouldn't have to do this with students. If it worked, the students who succeeded would talk about it enough to make it attractive to other students. Students who succeeded would quickly recognize that the ones who didn't like it were students who didn't want to do the work.

If implemented as explained in this book, far more students would hear about this new way to learn and want to try it than the other way around. Any school that tried the CBC would be wise to provide copies of this book for students to borrow. There is nothing in this book that secondary students and their parents could not understand. The more it is explained to interested students and the more they get a chance to try it, the more successful it will be and the more quickly it can get started.

To answer critics who ask how the CBC can be evaluated, the answer is simple: use the state test scores. If the method works, increased state test scores will be the fairest way to judge its effectiveness. My experience in the GSQ's is there should be an increase after one full year in any CBC classroom. State test scores are now stagnant in the secondary schools; this would help them break out of that difficulty. I think both students and parents, *especially in disadvantaged neighborhoods*, will ask for CBC's. In over forty years of working in the schools, I haven't seen any other approach that has the potential of the CBC for raising the competence of students to the levels they need for success in life.

In this chapter, I will focus on the required academic subjects: English which includes reading and, especially, writing, math, science, history and social studies. This doesn't mean teachers of other subjects could not teach this way, but since these are basic subjects with which I am very familiar, I will address them here. But as I have already explained, speaking, listening and problem solving are core subjects in a CBC and are an integral part of everything taught in these classes.

Because of the unique way students are evaluated in a CBC—individual conferences between students and teachers or TA's—a lot of focus will be on both writing and problem solving. Since success on the achievement tests is highly correlated with those two skills very quickly state test scores would rise.

Beginning the Year - General Suggestions

If you decide to teach a CBC whether as an experiment for a few weeks or for a year starting in

September, I suggest you introduce the ideas in this book to your students and their parents and allow a lot of time for discussion. If you are starting in the fall, you might say something like the following in your own words, "What I want to do this year is teach differently from the way I've been teaching and the way you've been learning. I call it the CBC or Competence Based Classroom approach. I'll begin today to explain it to you and I'd like it very much if you'd give it your best. As I told you when you showed interest, we'll give this method a five-week trial and then we'll re-evaluate. If most of you want to go on, the students who don't can go back to the regular program. I don't think I'll have any trouble replacing them with volunteers.

I also believe, because it's new and different, that a lot of students in the school are going to be skeptical about what goes on in the CBC. The first rumor that's going to spread through the school is, 'I hear in that class everyone gets a B whether they work or not.' I'm not worried about that. I'm going to let the state test scores decide how effective the CBC is. The results should be significant the first year. This is not an AP class but we may learn as much as they do if you are willing to cooperate."

What I've just written is only a suggestion. You may use it or, after reading this book, decide to paraphrase it in your own words. How much you use the rest of this chapter is up to you. But what you will be doing is moving from the old system of teaching, and, grading to the new way of teaching, testing and then re-teaching, using competence as the benchmark for when to go ahead.

Explain that competence or a B grade is the minimal standard for credit in a CBC and that you will be the sole judge of what is competent work. Explain that you are flexible. If the student can make a good argument that what he or she has been doing deserves credit, you'll listen. But there will be no credit for less than competent work. This means the ABCDF grading system will not be in use. The lowest grade for credit will be a B. An A or higher is also possible but we'll talk further about that when we get to the end of the first unit of work.

There will be no failure or F grades. If a student does not do competent work, he or she will receive an incomplete which can only be changed if the unit is completed at the level of competence required for credit. If a student receives an incomplete, you will work something out with him if he wants to raise the incomplete to a B.

Begin by explaining schooling and that there is no schooling in a CBC. Emphasize that all tests, written schoolwork and class discussions will be open-book or open discussion. Even during a test students may get help from you or from other students if they need it. Re-explain if necessary that the evaluation for competence is always the result of a conference between you or a TA and the student about his or her work. But no matter how long it takes, all assigned work, which includes the answer to every test question, would be checked off as competent or correct before it is accepted for credit. You would also explain that you would make every effort to help each student complete his or her work on time.

The CBC is a cooperative effort, not a competitive one. As in most well managed work places in the real world, students would not compete against other students. They would be encouraged to compete against their own previous performances or possibly as a group against similar classes in their school. Students in classes who thought the CBC was a free ride to a B, might challenge your class to a discussion about material both classes had covered. But when you make it clear to the challengers that there is no schooling in a CBC, they might back off. To be more authentic, the only challenge you would accept for your class would be on using knowledge, not on who had memorized the most.

You would explain that the CBC covers all the state and district requirements. The difference is that to get credit all the work needs to be done competently. You would, however, put no pressure on any student to do superior work or to work for an A. While a good class might accomplish more or individual students much more, this would be up to the individual students to decide if they wanted to work for more than competence. Teachers would keep records of the student's progress, but students would also keep individual records of what they have accomplished so that they would always know exactly where they stood in the process of getting credit for each course.

Educational vs. Non-Educational Competence

You would also explain something that would be very new to your beginning students: you will teach and test for *educational competence*. This is defined as: *using knowledge that can be improved*. Such knowledge requires thinking and then using the thinking in *speaking, listening, reading, writing and problem solving.* Your job will be to continually explain that while schooling is also knowledge, it is *non-educational* knowledge because *it can't be improved.*

As in the elementary school, there is also knowledge that may be required but this will diminish to a tiny amount as the students will have access to books, the Internet and to CD ROMS that are packed with information. But you will explain to them that information is only useful if it is used and, in the CBC, the test for knowledge is: *Can it be both used and improved?*

Therefore, in a CBC, students would be asked to check calculations, spelling, and facts for accuracy in order to get credit on tests, assignments, and where appropriate, in classroom discussions. For example, once they have proven to the teacher they can do hand calculations, they will be encouraged to use a calculator. To get credit for spelling, all words spelled incorrectly would need to be corrected. But as in the real world, they would be encouraged to use dictionaries or spell-check programs. With enough practice, this *the-spelling-must-be-correct method*, will insure they spell much better than most do now by memorizing words out of context on spelling tests.

While all facts would need to be correct to get credit on both assigned work and tests, students will not be asked to memorize. Time would be spent teaching students where to look things up and, essentially, how to access information and check facts for accuracy. Since non-educational knowledge is finite and invariable, in a CBC, as in the real world, it would need to be accurate. But since it is knowable and accessible, non-educational knowledge would not be the focus of any major teaching or testing in a CBC.

It is obvious that any spelling words and facts that were used frequently would be memorized, as it is easier to memorize them than to keep looking them up. We commit to memory what we use frequently and what interests us. Unless we are forced, we do not commit to memory what interests others. In the CBC, you are free to teach as you would like to, to be creative and interesting. By setting the floor at competence and giving your students every chance to get there, you've done a lot more for many of them than school has ever done. But it's their responsibility to do the work.

If they complain the work is too hard, you can say all I'm asking of you is what supervisors are going to ask of you for the rest of your life: competence. In my education store, competence is the price for credit. I'll do all I can to help you afford that price. But I will not reduce it because, if I do, you'll suffer the same as you do whenever you buy something cheap that falls apart as soon as you try to use it. The price you'll pay is fair; please don't ask me to cheat you by reducing it.

CBC learning would depend on team effort.

I suggest CBC courses be divided into learning teams, with perhaps two, three or four students on each team, as is done now in most chemistry and physics courses. With your approval, students could choose who they want to work with and how many they would want on their team: two, three or four. The teams, however, need not be permanent. They could be changed throughout the year so that students could have a chance to be on teams with other members of the class. Students who do not want to work on a team would be allowed to work alone, but encouraged to contribute to the learning of the whole community in discussions and as TA's in order to feel included and connected.

The purpose of the teams would be to work and learn together on all assignments. Team members would both help and check each other making sure everyone is involved and current. But, since the students would be evaluated individually, students who did not work would not get credit for what other students did. In the parlance of cooperative learning, there would be no hitch-hiking.

Teachers would teach the whole class as much as they believed was necessary but, also, go from team to team both to assist team members or individuals working alone when they are stuck. When team members decided that they were ready to be checked after a test or an assignment, each would go individually to the teacher to be checked for competence. Once students were checked off as competent, they would have the option of helping other students on their team or going ahead on their own. Students would not be required to help others on their team once they were checked off.

If their team members give up trying to help them, students who were not competent would have to depend on you or on a student teacher-assistant or TA for help. Students who got so far behind that, in a reasonable time, neither the teacher nor the TA could bring them up to competence would be given an incomplete and would talk with the teacher about how the work could be completed. There would still be no failure but to get credit some students would have to repeat the course.

One of the major complaints of employers is that the students who come to work for them don't know how to work together on a team. The CBC teams are the best possible preparation for this necessary life skill.

Judy Barnes Claps recalls how she implemented this concept:

As a classroom teacher, I approached my students on an individual basis, but I also viewed my role as promoting "family" relationships. Since I taught inner city middle school, my students quickly made it abundantly clear that their primary concerns were peer acceptance and peer relationships. Classroom learning took a definite back seat. Although I might become personally important to each student, it was made clear that our relationship was secondary to that with their peers. (Early in my career I had a student tell me that he would not excel in reading because his friends would no longer accept him if he did well.) Therefore, my role became to focus on building positive interactions within the group which included me as a member. I also learned to build a strong, personal relationship with the parents because their attitude towards me and the school directly influenced the attitude of their children. This was especially important in an area where so many of the parents had not had a good experience in school themselves. All of this is to explain why I think that one must use a slightly different emphasis when working in a school than in a counseling situation. It is more of a system approach, more of what one would do in family therapy.

In an excerpt from a paper she wrote called "Increasing Participatory Management in the Classroom" Judy describes the system she used.

As the students entered the classroom, they were seated in eight learning teams of three or four students each. The grading system was explained and a great deal of emphasis was placed on the fact that they would be in these groups for eight weeks and therefore had to learn to get along with each other and work as a unit. Each of the groups chose a name and did a series of non-academic team-building activities. Each activity was debriefed and plans were made to strengthen weak areas. At the end of two days, the teams made up songs, cheers, or raps. It was interesting and gratifying to note that all of them emphasized the things they would do together as well as individual strengths.

At the beginning of the first full week of school the task rotation was begun.

The purpose of these jobs was to shift as much control of the classroom as possible from the teacher to the students, to make students responsible for actually running the program.

Group One was in charge of administering the spelling test, grading it, and re-testing any students until all had grades of 80% or better. This turned out to be a major task since the class was weak in this area.

Group Two was in charge of reviewing what had been covered in mathematics that week and creating a review test by noon Thursday which they would submit for teacher review. The test would be administered, graded and re-test given when necessary by the group.

Group Three had the responsibility for writing, administering, grading, and re-testing for the week's work in Social Studies.

Group Four was in charge of finding four poems of differing genre to present orally to the group. Needless to say, a lot of poetry was read while making their selections.

Group Five was in charge of presenting a summary of current events for the week. The group opted to use a television format and it caught on. There was a balance among national, local, school, and personal news without prompting.

Group Six was in charge of room maintenance, such as keeping the floor and blackboards clean, watering the plants, straightening shelves, and generally keeping the room tidy.

Group Seven was in charge of collecting homework, distributing papers and supplies. Eventually they took over the responsibility of collecting reading response journals in the form of letters to classmates and acting as mailmen.

Group Eight had to prepare or buy a snack, advertise it, and sell it on Friday. This ten minute activity helped them to learn the concepts of gross and net profit, overhead, and optimum price. It was a nice break and the profits went towards classroom special events.

By establishing these rotating tasks, the students were given control over their tests, learned a valuable study and review technique, and a considerable portion of routine grading and re-testing was shifted away from the teacher. This enabled her to concentrate her time on the evaluation of writing, which is an extremely time-consuming task. More important, it allows a single teacher without support personnel to test and re-test, thus giving every student the opportunity to reach a competency level of 80% or better. This makes the students realize that they are important, as is the material to be learned. They know the teacher will not just move on leaving the impression that it is all right if they do not understand the material.

This program takes time, but the resulting reduction in classroom stress and the increase in positive academic and social growth makes it all worth the effort. The students in this classroom accepted tests as a normal part of learning and study without nervousness or cramming at the last minute. There is no fear of failure because they know they can take the test again if necessary. If anything, they are a bit too casual about the tests. The students were amazingly fair in their composition and grading of tests. They took responsibility without being reminded. There were short class meetings every third day in which problems were resolved and plans made for on-going projects and upcoming events. The students learned to back up their opinions and argue rationally in defense of their points of view in disagreements with other students and adults. They knew the program had enough flexibility to adjust if there was a demonstrably valid reason. This gave them a real sense of power and control.

In this paper, Judy says, "I have described what can be done in a self-contained classroom. However, this can be modified to work in a departmental situation by having the student groups responsible for writing a segment of the test or a type of question for the test. Thematic instruction can be used to foster communication and cooperation between different teachers who work with the same group of students."[5]

A Sample Assignment in Writing

Writing well is a very important competence in a CBC. A sample writing assignment in English, social studies, history and science (all of which require competent writing), would be to ask students to read a passage in the text (or any place else) and to write a short, one-page critique of what they read. In the beginning, the CBC would stress short, competent writing. The ability to write does not improve by writing a lot of pages poorly. For competence, it would be better to work on one short assignment for a long time rather than produce several less competent assignments over the same span of time.

The students would work individually to write the critique and then, in their team, check what each has written and make suggestions to improve what each other wrote. Students would not have to accept these suggestions but they would be encouraged to listen to what was offered. The teacher would give them a time limit for completing the assignment. For the first and second writing assignments, the teacher would go over each critique for competence and point out where it needed to be improved, including correcting errors of spelling, grammar and fact. Until it was both competent and correct, it would not be checked off.

From this early writing, the teacher would learn who in the class was a competent writer and select these students to be TA's who would then be able to help check other students' writing. The teacher would spot check all the work of the TA's and also check the work of any student who wanted or needed to be checked by the teacher instead of a TA. With the help of the TA's, the teacher would have more time than now to work with individual students or with student teams. Volunteering as a TA would be a way to earn an A as described in Chapter Eight.

A TA would also tutor students if he or she had the time. The teacher would continually search for more TA's as it is common knowledge that the best way to learn is to teach. This means the TA's would help but they would profit from this help as much as the students they tutored. All students would be asked to explain or "defend" what they had written to the teacher and/or to the TA so that it was certain that the writing was original with the writer and that he or she understood why what they wrote was competent. Defending their work would give the students much needed practice in speaking and listening.

Since competent writing that can be defended is half the skill of using language (with speaking and listening the other half), a great deal of time and effort would be put into teaching all students to write well the first year they were in any CBC except math. Since *competent reading* is required to pass all CBC tests, as well as all standard achievement tests, the best way by far to learn to read well is to learn to write well.

Class Discussion in History, Social Studies, English and Science

There would be much less lecturing in a CBC than is done now in regular classes. Since all the students would focus on learning to write and through that learning, to read competently, discussions based on reading in class and at home would be a major way to improve learning. Students would not be individually evaluated on their discussions, as this might inhibit participation, but the teacher would comment on the creativity and originality of the discussions as a whole. Once students gained skill in discussion, they would be encouraged to lead. This is also a very important life skill that few students in today's classes have a consistent opportunity to practice. Leading discussions would always be voluntary; no student would ever be required to lead.

Homework in a CBC

Most homework assigned today in secondary schools is not done competently except in upper tracks and AP Classes. Homework done incompetently is worse than no homework at all. Therefore, most homework in a CBC would be self-assigned in that students who were struggling for competence on a test or other assignments would not be given class time to do the work they had to complete for credit. The pressure on them would be their desire for credit.

Assigned homework would mostly be reading to prepare for classwork, especially, for class discussions or to answer teacher or student questions about what they were assigned. This way the teacher could easily see by the students' participation in discussions or their ability to answer questions whether they did the assignment or not. Any written homework would be checked off for competence by the teacher or TA just the same as work done in class. If the written work was not competent their homework would again be to do what was necessary to bring it up to snuff.

Testing In History, Social Studies, English and Science

Essentially, all tests would be open book and open to getting any help the students needed. The idea is for each student to put as much as she can of what she's learned into answering questions competently. You would not be concerned about how the student got the knowledge, but you would very much care that the student could explain and defend what was written on her paper in the personal evaluation conferences.

Emphasis on using what has been learned is not a common school experience even though it's been the core of learning since the beginning of time. By the end of their first year in any CBC, the students may be exposed to more personal teacher-student interaction than they have had since they left the primary grades. You can be free to take your time; this student-teacher interaction is critical to learning how to learn and to appreciating learning. Success here for any student, especially for disadvantaged students, could turn them on to learning for the rest of their lives.

To be competent, *all* test questions would either have to be answered correctly, assuming of course, that there were correct answers or, if there were no correct answers, in the judgment of the teacher, answered competently. You would be continually looking for answers that showed the student was improving and you would make it a point to comment on this improvement. It is obvious there could be no cheating in a CBC. What would ordinarily be called cheating in school would be encouraged because in the end, each individual would be given the time to explain to you what she knows and how she can use what she knows.

Students who believed they had written highly competent answers might ask to be checked first. If the teacher believes their answers show a superior understanding of the work, they would be asked to act as TA's for that test. That way they could assist the teacher in checking other tests and free the teacher to work with students or teams who were having difficulty achieving competence. Given the help of the TA's, teaching could move along quickly and students would still get a lot of personal attention. All students would have teacher assigned or self-selected topical reading, writing or independent studies to work on while the tests or other assignments were being evaluated. This time would be planned so that the students would look forward to it and come prepared to do it.

Students who needed more time to complete their test to the competence level would do so on their own as homework or in study halls. Team members, tutors and parents would be encouraged to help students with test questions. As in every assignment, all questions on every test would have to be checked for accurate facts and correct spelling to get credit. There would be no exceptions.

Obviously, the teacher would need to start slowly and gradually raise the level of what was defined as competent. By slowly building a good foundation, students later on would be able to proceed more quickly. By the end of the first year in a CBC, the level of competence should be much higher than at the beginning.

This is not running in place as often happens in schools where students are excessively schooled. Schooling can be increased but, since it is not educational knowledge, it can't be improved. In these required subjects, many of the test questions would be gleaned from a wide variety of multiple-choice questions found on sample standardized achievement tests such as state achievement tests, the ACT and SAT or from any other available standardized tests. This method of testing would not only help students learn what you are teaching but would also give every student much needed practice in answering these questions correctly. There is no guessing in a CBC; students would learn a lot about how to do well on these important tests.

With this one exception, all other tests would be teacher-constructed and all would be teacher or TA checked for an explanation of anything that wasn't obviously correct or competent on the written page. The one exception to the above would be that any competent student who wished to construct additional test questions to show a greater understanding of the material would be encouraged to do so. These extra questions could then be answered by the students who wrote them to raise their grades to A or A+ depending on the teacher's judgment.

Based again on the teacher's judgment, these extra questions could be put in a pool that other students could select from while others' tests were being evaluated. They could also be taken home for homework to give them an opportunity to raise their grade from competent to superior or an A. Additionally, they could be used by the students who created them to lead a discussion that might interest other students in the class. All students would be encouraged to do extra work in their interest area to raise their grades above competence. This would be the ongoing challenge of the CBC's.

Lateral Work in History, Social Studies, English and Science

There would be times when the work got so difficult that some students would be stuck for a while and it would make no sense to go ahead without them. Those who were ready would be given the opportunity to explore other areas laterally at the same level or pursue the same material in greater depth through independent study. This would give them a chance to be creative, to learn more and still stay with the bulk of the class. Instead of going ahead, some of the TA's who enjoyed tutoring might elect to tutor some of the stuck students individually or in small groups. The teacher would do what was needed to keep the process going, mostly working with the students who were having difficulty but also advising the students who were going laterally or in greater depth, and also encouraging others who were competent to tutor.

Math in a CBC Middle School

In a CBC math would be taught much differently than it is now. There would be no attempt to teach eighth grade math or ninth grade algebra. In math, which is very specifically set up to move from lower to higher levels, for example, from recognizing numbers to advanced calculus, right now we have a one-size-fits-all approach. That only works for the few students who fit the size exactly. Math is the one subject that does not have to be taught in homogeneous groups. Even if you could find a group of students who were all at the same place, there is no way you could keep them all at the same place. So it makes no sense to start that way.

No matter what happened in the elementary school, and this would be extremely variable, any middle school math teacher who wanted to create a CBC in math would start by assessing each student who entered his or her class to find out where they were in understanding math. It would make no difference what their record showed unless it was from a CBC math class—just find out what they know now. There are a variety of ways to do this, all available to the teacher. The simplest way is to use a good text that covers the span of where students might be and locate where they are on the math continuum.

For many students, even if they had previously received good grades, this level would be much lower than where the students thought they were. If the teacher started students too low, they could move rapidly up to where they belonged. If started so high, they couldn't do the work, you would adjust them down to where they could. There is nothing precise about this assessment. Just find a place where they could easily do the work and take it from there. If they spend a week or two reviewing, all the better. While this process would take some time, it is a necessary prelude to starting math in a CBC. This way of teaching works well because math is much more related to innate ability than other subjects. In the end you either know it or you don't. Unlike English or history, effort may not do very much for students who don't have the ability to do math.

Therefore, there is no sense trying to teach a class of students who are at different levels as we often do now. Once assessed, each student would be assigned to a group loosely based on that assessment. In the middle school some might be as high as algebra, while others might have difficulty with simple number recognition. But wherever they are, that is where they should start.

Students who are at the same level might begin by sitting together, but since they would learn at different rates, it would not make much sense to keep them together once they started to progress at their own speed. What would be necessary is that the teacher develop a system so students could keep track of where they were on the math continuum at any time during the year. Having a chart posted on the wall showing the math continuum of ability for the students to see will help them keep their own record of where they are.

To begin, the teacher would give the student a lot of work at the student's initial level so that he would gain confidence in his ability to solve problems at that level. For many, this initial level would be in the area of hand calculation. The key would be for the teacher to check each student, from the beginning to the end, using problems at that level. The student would have to explain to the teacher why he did what he did and how he got the answer. The teacher would ask him to do this until she was sure he understood and could do math at that level. When he could, he'd move up.

Basically all students would be required to be competent in using decimals, percentages, fractions, and simple story problems that required their use. Once students mastered the problems solved by hand calculation, fractions, decimals, and percentages first without and then with a calculator, they would go on to real educational (improvable) math, which would include solving story problems. Taught this way, I could see many capable middle school students gaining enough confidence so that by the end of the seventh grade they could be well into algebra and most of these students could finish and go beyond by the end of the eighth grade. All along, the teacher would explain to students the type of story problems best solved by the math at that level. Doing this would answer the question that many students ask now: *Where will I ever use this?* This is a method of teaching math I have seen used in schools where I've consulted and it works well.

But capable or not, moving students along in math in a CBC is simple and clear-cut. It is important that they be able to demonstrate individually to the teacher or to a TA that they can solve the math problems, including the story problems, at each ascending level of mathematics, and explain what they did and how they got the answers. Following a good math text until the end would set the levels for each student.

Some students would not get very far but at least they would be competent at some level. Many of them now are not competent at any level. A few would be so good at math that they ought to be put into special math classes and not be held back as they are now. For these students who have up until now been tied to seat time, there is no problem with competence, only boredom. Moving them ahead would solve that problem.

In math, giving homework would be for practice after they understood what they were doing. Students would not go on to new material unless they had competently demonstrated in class what they had been taught. Nothing turns students off more than being assigned math problems they don't know how to solve with no one at home to help them.

Math in High School

The high school CBC math teachers would do essentially the same for entering students as the middle school teachers did. They would check the level of competence of each entering student and would not take the word of, or accept the record of any student. Just because they are in the ninth or tenth grade does not mean they are ready for algebra or geometry. Once the level of competence is determined, each student would go on from there and be individually checked at each level by the teacher or a math TA. Math TA's would be selected from highly competent students the same as in any other class. Teachers would be cautious and err on the side of the student staying a little longer at a level when there was any question of competence.

If two years of math (algebra and geometry) are required, it is likely that many high school students in a

CBC would exceed these requirements before the end of two years. If they could pass a test that demonstrated their competence in both algebra and geometry, they should go on and get as far as they can in the two mandatory years. Many would get through advanced algebra or further in this time. If they had teachers who were skilled in explaining math and they elected to take three or four years of math, they should be well into calculus or even beyond by the time they graduated from high school.

The success of math in high school CBC's is predicated on the assumption that all math teachers would be able to teach a wide range of math levels in one class and keep moving students up in that class. They just shouldn't be moved ahead, no matter what grade they are in, until they are ready. But once students progressed into higher math such as analytical geometry, it would make sense to eliminate the lower math levels from these advanced classes.

There is an unsolvable problem with math in or out of the CBC

No matter what we do, there are a few people who are never going to get past simple arithmetic no matter how well we teach. If they have to pass algebra or geometry competently, they can't seem to do it. I have no solution for these students. We can ruin their lives by asking the impossible or we can give them a high school diploma by awarding them credit for basic arithmetic courses such as business math. Math literacy is not needed for most of the jobs in the world. Some of these people do well in jobs where they learn to use math through practical application such as in construction work.

The Future of CBC's

If the CBC's work as I expect they will, more and more students will want to get involved and more and more teachers will volunteer to teach in this satisfying way. Discipline problems will rarely occur in these classes because of the intense student-student interaction in their teams and the satisfying student-teacher interactions as all proceed to the level of competence or beyond. Also, because they are learning what is useful to know in the real world, competent students who know what they are doing and why they are doing it, will not act up.

The CBC approach, which stresses competence and intense non-coercive student-teacher involvement, will allow dedicated teachers to enjoy teaching. Many, if not all students, who decide to enter these classrooms will demonstrate that they are internally motivated, competent learners. When almost all the classes in a middle school or high school are CBC's, that school should be ready to declare itself a Glasser Quality School.

Nothing that I have written in this chapter takes precedence over the good judgment of any teacher. The goal is total student competence plus a lot of quality work. I welcome suggestions from any teacher that would improve what I have written here.

Ten

Teaching the Joy of Reading

When you look at a group of young children streaming happily into an elementary school in the morning, it's hard to realize that, for many of them, the joy you see is short-lived. In their classes, as more and more constraint is put on teachers to teach them to read, the teachers find it almost impossible to avoid pressuring the children to read faster and to understand more of what they read. If the goal of this pressure is to help the children to score higher on state achievement tests, many younger children are reading better. But if the goal of this pressure is to start them on the road to life-long reading, it is an abysmal failure.

All over the country, as this pressure on teachers continues to escalate, they are finding it harder and harder to do what most know is necessary if the children are to become life-long readers: *concurrently teach the children that the reward for making an effort to read is joy*. There is little joy for anyone, children or teachers, in the high pressure *reading-for-better-test-scores* classes that now dominate our elementary schools.

Improving reading test scores is reasonable. But improving them at the expense of long term learning is not, because reading is the core of all education. It is not the fault of the state reading tests that many children learn to hate reading. The fault is in how we use the tests and the external control used to try to increase the scores. In a GQS, the children learn both to read well and to enjoy doing it. Since they enjoy reading, they don't mind the tests and do well on them as was true at Aikman where they went from the 5th percentile to the 90th percentile and where all you see is joy. The mother who wrote the letter about her first grader's experience with reading pressure has a right to become concerned that her child is learning to hate reading.

Older students' reading scores do not change much after they get into secondary school. If they are good readers, mostly they'll stay good readers and vice versa. These mature students, who most need to experience joy if they are to be motivated to improve their reading don't find much joy from the C's and D's more than half of them earn in English in the secondary school. Without this joy to motivate them, they read only what is assigned and many of them don't read that.

We don't have the data yet to know whether the improvement at the primary grades are going to be maintained through graduation. But we do know that reading is a skill that needs practice if it is to be improved. There is no indication that C and D secondary school students are getting this practice by reading for pleasure any more than they ever did. Most of them never read again for pleasure. It is in the disadvantaged neighborhoods that the pressure to read does its greatest harm to motivation.

In the June 2000 issue of the Kappan is what I consider a heart breaking article titled, *Creating New Inequalities - Contradictions of Reform*.[6] There Linda M. McNeil writes about what is happening now in

Texas where the pressure to improve TAAS reading scores at an early age has become relentless, especially, in poor, minority neighborhoods. In this meticulously researched article using actual data from the Texas State Education Department, McNeil observes that, despite reading scores on the TAAS going up over the last ten years, graduation rates for minorities, Latinos and African Americans, are moving in the opposite direction.

The following data from the Texas Department of Education clearly shows that reading score increases are not translating into increased graduation rates for any students but, the greatest reduction is in the graduation rates of minority students. In 1978, before the big push for reading and better education was started by H. Ross Perot and increased each year since, the graduation rate for minority students was 60%. For whites that year it was 75%, a 15% disparity.

By 1990, the graduation rate for whites had dropped to 70% and the rates for minorities had dropped to 50%. Now the difference between white and minority, (70% vs 50%) had increased to 20%. But by 1999, the graduation rate for whites had gone back up to 75% but the graduation rate for minorities stayed the same, 50%. Now the disparity between whites and minorities had increased to 25%. This disproves the claim that the recent push in reading education is benefiting minorities as well as whites.

McNeil's extensive research also shows that despite increases in reading scores, there is nothing to show that minority students are actually reading faster or better than before the push to raise test scores in reading started. If graduation is any criteria, they are reading less well than before. McNeil concludes that by focusing so much on improving their reading test scores, the students are learning to test better but not learning to read better.

In the Aikman school, which is filled with joy, the students who have made striking gains on the TAAS, have neither been tutored nor pressured to increase their scores. Along with being taught to read they are also learning the joy of reading. If the program in Aikman is continued into the next school, through the sixth grade, there is a good chance that these students will become life-long readers.

Unlike math, high achievement in reading is much more related to teachers' expectations than to students' innate ability. Our experience at Aikman and at the other GQS's, shows that the better the relationship the students have with their teachers, the more the students will accept their teachers' high expectations as their own. In too many schools where children are pushed hard and punished with low grades if they don't succeed, they lose their desire to meet their teacher's expectations of them. A GQS, however, does not run on expectations; it runs on competence. Where there is caring, success and joy, there is no need for pressure or frenetic cramming with test-taking skills.

In a GQS, students are told over and over from the day they enter school: *you have a lot to learn about reading but don't worry. You're going to have plenty of time, we'll help you and you'll have a lot of fun.* The teachers have learned to trust the process. They are not worried when a child doesn't learn as quickly or as competently as other children. But by the third or fourth grade, these early differences, more caused by different rates of maturity than by inability to learn, level off and almost everyone becomes a competent reader. For the few who are still behind, the only strategy for success is to continue the caring and foster the joy. Any attempt to increase the progress with pressure will create what is now being seen in Texas: better test scores, but no increase in the ability to read.

The unexpected success of the Harry Potter books shows that young people will read for fun. In summer 2000, I saw seven-year olds on television camped out in a bookstore waiting for the midnight release of the latest Potter book. When asked if they would actually read a 600 page book, they laughed and intimated that, if it were Harry Potter, they'd read a 1000 page book. I was so curious someone gave me the first book. I read it and enjoyed it.

Harry Potter lives in an external control world that pushes him around and killed his parents. But what makes him a hero is it fails to control him. He uses both his brains and magic to escape the external control that surrounds him to the frustration of his enemies and the delight of his readers. In these books, external control is personified as evil and Harry uses his magic to combat evil and win.

No one needs to pressure these young people to read these books. If anything, pressure may have to be applied to get them to put the books down and do their schoolwork or their chores. One thing that struck me as I watched the kids on television was that they were all Anglo or Asian. I did not see one African-American or Latino child. I don't know if these books have as much appeal to those groups as they do to the groups represented on television. But my guess is that this kind of book might have great appeal if it were introduced to minority children in school.

Here is a chance to get students to become competent readers at a cost of pennies compared to the high cost of the reading program described in Linda McNeil's article. But will we take advantage of this serendipitous opportunity and buy stacks of these compelling books for all schools and not short change the poor schools along the way? I wonder. If not, I believe it's another example of the system widening the gap between the haves and the have-nots.

Even though I explained an enjoyable way for students to memorize needed facts in Chapter Eight, there are limits to how much pleasure we can pack into learning facts. Reading is just the opposite. As Harry Potter shows, you have to work hard to make a good book unenjoyable. There are plenty of good books, Harry Potter is not the only hero around. We have to work to get some of them not only into the classroom but also into students' homes. We talk a lot about improving reading; buying good books and letting children take them home to read will do more than anything we are doing now. It's time to put our money where our mouth is.

For a hundred years or more, teachers have used a variety of rewards and punishments to try to motivate students to read. Mostly, the children resist. For example, the most commonly used method of teaching reading—dividing a class into three reading groups—is good practice as long as they are not divided into levels like high, middle and low. The high and middle are not so bad but being in the low group sends the you-are-less-than-competent message, a message that destroys motivation whenever and wherever it is sent. If you want to use reading groups, don't organize them by levels. Mix them up, read a lot to the children and ask the better readers to help the ones who need help.

Many students who don't read well resent the pressure all around them at school and even at home to get more involved in reading. They resist this pressure in a variety of ways. The current and most popular is to stop paying attention and get labeled ADD to escape the pressure. But the labeling has a downside. It sends students the message that there is something wrong with their brains, not a good message to send to anyone.

Improved reading is worth the challenge but it will take time. If we try to hurry the process with pressure, we lose. In helping these children catch on to the joy of reading, you are fighting for their educational lives. There is absolutely nothing better to do with your time than to read a good book to a child. That minimal effort is the strongest weapon you have to work against the *give up, we can't do it or we're not very good at it mentality* that locks poor readers into low school achievement and failure. This can escalate to a neighborhood mentality, a minority mentality, or a gender mentality commonly seen in boys who are slow in reading and who see girls reading faster.

If you use a method to teach, be creative and vary the method. Teach your students very long words like Mississippi because long words are easier to recognize than short words and they'll think recognizing a long word is a big deal. Don't try to motivate them with non-reading rewards like candy or smiling faces as this denigrates the actual value of their reading. Use the natural rewards of more time with you, or time with an aide, or a volunteer whose main job is to read them interesting stories.

Try theatrical methods. Find a simple script and cast them in a play. They don't have to memorize the script. This is not a performance. Reading the script is exactly what you want them to do. Give a poor reader, a couple of funny lines and he'll be hooked on looking for more. Maybe the play has a tongue twister like Blue Bugs Blood that he repeats throughout and it makes all the students laugh. Then go from there to talking about tongue twisters and why they're so hard to say. Invite the students to make up their own tongue twisters and write them on the board for all the class to read and enjoy.

Ask around for suggestions from other teachers. Play reading games where there are teams, not individual students, so that even the slow reader on the team can win as the team wins; as he wins he will become a better reader. Have the teams decipher hard sentences or guess the best words to fill in a blank. Children love games. Just make sure there are no regular losers. Read the same book over and over until the students know all the words. Then when they are sick of it, threaten them with reading it again. And when they groan, admit that you're tired of it too and go on to a new book. It's your interaction with them when they have no chance to lose or get a low grade, that will keep them reading and involved. Vary your teaching. Don't worry so much about it being interesting for them. Worry about making it interesting for you. They'll soon be gone; you may be doing this for next thirty years. Believe me, if it's interesting for you, it'll be even more interesting for them because it's new. Find some things the slower readers are good at, like running fast or doing somersaults or making funny faces so you can balance the bad feelings they may have by not being as good at reading with the good feelings of showing what they can do well. This doesn't sound like much but it keeps the idea front and center in their minds that, if they can do anything well, they can also learn to read well.

Remember, reading is closely related to speaking and make sure that you encourage your slower readers to talk in class. Tell them: *if you can learn to speak a word, you can learn to read a word. It's the same word, whether it comes out of your mouth or it's written on a piece of paper.* Play the game of asking your students to listen for new words as you teach. When they hear one, tell them to let you know and then make a list of the new words they've discovered on the board with their initials after their word.

Use homonyms like pair, pear and pare and play games with them. What you are doing is more than teaching them to read. You are introducing them to the language. Spend time on slang and enlist their expertise because here they'll know a lot more than you do. Teach them the words of the seven deadly habits: criticizing, blaming, complaining, nagging, threatening, punishing and rewarding (to control). And then the connecting habits: caring, listening, supporting, contributing, encouraging, trusting and befriending that build strong relationships. Have circle-ups to discuss each of these connecting words and why they help you and your students connect.

Many of these suggestions may not be new to you. I don't claim to be an expert on reading. You may be an excellent teacher of reading and not be interested in any of what I've just suggested. My expertise is human relationships and the very harmful effect any sort of message that you are a failure has on each of us, young or old.

Students who are having difficulty in school know they are having difficulty. What they want from their teacher is what you wanted from your teachers when you were having difficulty, and what you wanted from your parents and your friends when you were having difficulty. Maybe what you want right now if you are having some difficulty with one of your children, your husband or your wife, is love.

I'm not talking about hugs and kisses even though hugs and kisses are great when appropriate. I'm talking about how you tell people who are having problems in school, out of school, anywhere, that you love them in ways that are appropriate to the situation. Talk to them about love and teach them the vocabulary of love. Doing this is good for them but it's good for you, too. No one is ever harmed by getting too much love no matter what kind it may be.

Read to them about love. Whenever I think about love, *Charlotte's Web*, the book by E.B. White comes to mind. I read that book to my four-year old son a hundred nights in a row and, at the end, when Charlotte died, we cried every time.

Eleven

Connecting Replaces Disciplining

As they are used in schools, discipline programs are totally external control because inherent in the word discipline is do what has to be done to make students obey, essentially, coerce or punish. "I can't teach them until I get them settled down" is the refrain I hear over and over when I meet with teachers. But don't get me wrong, this is a legitimate complaint. Teaching is hard enough when all students are in good order. In a GQS, no student has the right to remain in class if he behaves in a way that is harmful to others or disrupts the teaching. But as long as a student is not in any way disruptive, the student should not be removed even if he or she makes no attempt to learn. That behavior answers the Harrington condition: *they are there*. It is up to the teachers to reach them and teach them.

There are two kinds of student behavior that concern teachers. The first and most common is what I call *incident behaviors* such as students talking, arguing, scuffling, littering, occasionally being late for class, etc. In these, *there is no premeditated attempt by the student to disrupt the class or make trouble in the school*. These students are not disconnected. Their infractions are usually small, time-limited power struggles that crop up naturally when young people get together both in and out of school. If dealt with early enough by asking for cooperation without using external control, few of these students will ever have to be removed from class.

If the incidents become too numerous, they need to be handled by giving the involved student some attention. This is where the circle-ups can be used to solve the problem along with brief choice theory conversations aimed not so much at the incident as at improving the connection between the students and whomever has to deal with them. All the teachers could benefit from some training that gives them practice in how to do this. (See Appendix B)

For the most part, by the time the school is running without any external control, nothing more is needed than a brief reminder along with talking it over using the seven connecting or choice theory habits that build strong relationships: *caring, listening, supporting, contributing, encouraging, trusting and befriending.*

The second, less common, but much more serious, incidents are what I call *problem behaviors.* These are the whole gamut of behaviors where disconnected students make a premeditated effort to disrupt the functioning of the school, mostly in class but often out of class. Problem incidents in class should be handled as I suggested you handle Tom in Chapter Three. Often, students like Tom come to school from homes where they have less than satisfying connections with even one parent. They may have connections to other young people like themselves, as in gangs, but these connections are rarely used for anything more than lashing out at a world full of people with whom they cannot connect.

Tom's humming was hardly an isolated incident. If you go back into his records, you will see that he has been exhibiting problem behaviors for a long time: it is

a record of the constant activity of a seriously disconnected student. When he behaves the way he usually
does, he has always been disciplined. He knows
nothing but external control and his disruptive behaviors are his way of using external control on others
no matter how much harm it does to the satisfying relationships he needs. In his mind, he doesn't care. He
can't destroy his good relationships; he has none to
destroy.

The only way you and the staff of your school can
succeed with Tom is to figure out how to connect with
him or reconnect with him assuming that at one time,
maybe as long ago as the primary grades, he was connected with a teacher. To do that you have to give up
using external control with Tom even if he continues to
use it with you. There is no other way. Tom will not
help you. He'll keep using external control on you and
others until he gets connected. Even though it doesn't
seem that he does, he needs you more than the connected students. But he doesn't know he needs you.
He's been exposed to so many years of external
control, that he has no more than a dim awareness of
what he's missing.

It is at this point the CBC is so critical because the
only way you can succeed with him is if he actually experiences real school success. Getting rid of the
external control alone will not do it. It was school
success, combined with good relationships, when previously there had been only school failure and
disconnection, that made the program at the Ventura
School so effective.

If you could go back and talk to the teachers who
taught Tom when he was in the primary grades, many
of them might say, "He was a little trouble but mostly

he was an interesting, curious child." Most of the Toms in our schools are created by the sudden increase in external control that they may experience after the primary grades, especially, after they arrive in middle school.

One of the experiences that leads teachers to believe external control is effective is that punishment does work if the students who are punished feel connected to their teacher or even if they don't, they feel strongly connected at home. For these students, who may occasionally be involved in annoying behaviors, the punishment they are threatened with such as the teacher saying, "Please stop doing what you're doing and settle down or your grades will suffer," is very effective. It is effective because these connected students want to learn and do well. They experience punishment as a reminder, not as an attempt to hurt them.

Jaime Escalante, the great calculus teacher of the movie, *Stand and Deliver*, was such a teacher. He was able to get away with what looked like a lot of external control because he convinced his students he cared about them and what he taught would help them to succeed in life. But it's a lot easier to get rid of the external control than to depend on your ability to use the deadly habits on your students and still stay connected with them.

Dealing with the disconnected students who repeatedly choose problem behaviors

Problem students are already disconnected. There is no other solution to the way they behave except to do all that you can do to connect with them. Research shows[7] clearly that, even if the student is disconnected at home, a successful connection with a teacher or teachers at school can work what may seem to be a small miracle.

For example, Claire, a student at Huntington Woods Elementary School, the first Glasser Quality School, was one of those miracles. She went from the over-whelming external control world she lived in including a mental health care facility to the total choice theory environment of Huntington Woods. This occurrence is described in the book, *Quality is the Key, Stories From Huntington Woods*, by Sally Ludwig and Kaye Mentley, the principal at that time.

CLAIRE: One Student's Story:

What can a school do to help an intelligent child who faces serious challenges in life? Eight-year-old Claire had been in a residential program for severely emotionally impaired children at a local mental health care facility. School principal Kaye Mentley tells that, upon her discharge, Claire's parents wanted to enroll her at Huntington Woods Elementary School.

Claire's symptoms were fairly classic for a di-agnosis of severe emotional impairment—lying, stealing, foul language, physical aggression. Her discharge recommendation called for a full-time placement in a room for severely emotionally im-paired children, with a maximum of nine other children, a full-time teacher, of course, a full-time instructional paraprofessional assigned to her, separate music class, separate recess, separate lunch from the rest of the students, an adult with her any time she was out of the classroom. And she was to see a school social worker twice a week. I said to Claire's mother, "You have to understand that if you enroll her here, she's not going to get any of that' She said, "yes, I understand. But we want to try it" so we agreed.

Two years after Claire came to Huntington Woods, Kaye Mentley was in the hallway one day talking with teachers visiting the school when Claire, now a fifth-grade student, came along the hall. Mrs. Mentley called her over and said:

Claire, I know this is short notice, but since you are going to speak at the conference next week, would you talk with these visitors? What are you going to tell people at the conference when they ask about your experience at our school?

Claire replied:

Well, I'm going to tell them that I came here and I have completely turned around, I used to be in, like, a mental hospital. I used to lie and steal. I was mouthy. I don't do that anymore. Mrs. Mentley knows that I can still act like a brat at times, but I'm working on that. I have goals in my life now and I'm not going to be like that.

One of the visiting teachers asked, "Have you changed as a person since you've been here?" Claire answered:

Yes, This school helped me change my whole life. Before, at my other schools, I was a horrible student. I was always getting mad, and when I got mad I would steal and lie. I didn't get much attention, so I felt like if I stole then maybe I'd get a little attention. All they gave me was time out or a grounding or even a detention or a suspension. So I went through counseling at school, but that didn't help. The schoolwork we did was really boring because I would do the same work over and over again. I used to have to do stuff in third grade that I did in first. I didn't like it and neither did my mom.

And then I came here— the teachers and students helped me so I wouldn't do those things. I got more attention and I told myself I didn't have to do it anymore, getting in trouble. If I got grouchy my teachers told me to calm down, work the problem out, don't fight, just solve it by talking. And that really helped me a lot. It's been two and a half years since I've done the things I used to do. They helped me and now I can evaluate my behavior and figure out how to do better. I'm doing great here. I wish this school went through college.

Claire's home life is still very difficult, but she is happy and successful, especially at school. A visitor who knew of her history could not pick her out of her learning family. Now, she has made many friends, and loves to go into the preschoolers' room to help the teacher with young children. She is one of our student leaders, and is a student host, speaking to adult audiences. She has mastered all of her grade level standards and is working on those for the sixth and seventh grades. One of Claire's teachers, Sandy Hartman, said:

Claire is another child we have seen absolutely blossom here. Within the first few months after she came to Huntington Woods, most of the behaviors that had previously been labeled as severe emotional impairment disappeared. Some old learned behaviors might creep in once in a while, but she, the child who wasn't helpful and wanted nothing to do with anyone, and was street wise and knew it all — real tough — has grown tremendously. She is helpful now, and loves to help with little ones. She is a wonderful writer, and is able to express a lot of her feeling in writing. Now, she is speaking for Huntington Woods, going to make public presentations with teachers and with Kaye, and talking with visitors. Her power is coming in a positive way, and she knows she does not need that other kind of power. She doesn't need to do the things she did before to meet her needs. It has been fun, and fascinating, watching her change.

What does it take for a child to change direction as Claire has? At Huntington Woods School, we believe that every child can achieve quality learning and gain effective control of his or her life in an environment that provides the right conditions. In a Quality School, the entire system is designed to help all its students improve their lives through learning — learning the information, skills, and values that will help them live successfully and responsibly, now and in the future. Our goal is to help students to achieve their highest potential and develop personal responsibility and self-control, not by coercion, threats, or rewards, but by teaching them to fulfill their basic human needs in responsible, effective ways, and to solve problems by talking them through.

In a Glasser Quality School an attempt is made to teach all students and all interested parents choice theory.

As you start to use these ideas, begin teaching your class or classes some choice theory. Again a little training will help you to do this but all you really have to do to prepare for this beginning effort is read the first three chapters of the book, *Choice Theory*. That much will get you started. Later you might want to read more of *Choice Theory* as you continue to use these ideas. You need not devote much time to this effort. Keep it casual, maybe once or twice a week for five or ten minutes, talk to them enough to get them interested, but not so much that they see it as work. As you go along, emphasize that we all choose everything we do and we can always make better choices. Ask your students to explain the choice theory they learn to their parents and make an hour or two of parent training available at the school for parents who want more.

On your own, you can start by explaining the basic needs, especially the need for love and belonging and how we all need each other. Then explain how the need for power can mess up our relationships. Point out to them that what you've just explained is the reason you don't punish. You don't want them to see you as running a power trip on them and it's normal to resist power. It is this attempt to control them and their resistance to it that will harm your relationships and make things worse.

Explain that when people are getting along well with each other they feel as if they're connected, a feeling based on trusting and helping each other. Tell them that you want to be connected with all of them and, if you punish them, you'll never make that connection. If they are interested as most will be, you can explain more. Students are rarely taught the reason for anything the teacher does and you will find they are very interested in what you have to say. I'm just making these suggestions to get you started.

A fun way to teach elementary school students choice theory is to offer them the activities described in *My Quality World Workbook* by Carleen Glasser, my wife. There are also versions designed for Middle School and Early Childhood Education.

In a Glasser Quality School, The Connecting Place is used instead of the principal's office for students who are sent from class.

Once a staff led by the principal decides to move toward a GQS, there should be a place where students can be sent in which a staff member can work with them and try to connect with them. This can be a room, if one is available or any other place in the school where students can go until they can be sent back to class. If the school makes a serious effort to get rid of external control and implements the CBC, the room may not be necessary for much more than a year. But there should always be a place where a staff member such as a counselor or a trained aide can take an upset student, keep him for a while, calm him down by reaching out to him and then, with the permission of his teacher, send him back to class.

As stated in Chapter Three, if the student is sent to The Connecting Place or even to the office before The Connecting Place is established, it is best if the teacher who sends him, comes there and talks with him before taking him back. This does not have to be a fixed practice. The staff member or aide who runs The Connecting Place could, with the teacher's permission, send the student back without the teacher coming to the room.

If the teacher sends a student such as Tom to The Connecting Place she might say, "We have a new room called The Connecting Place. Remember we've been talking in class about connecting and I don't think we're connected. I'd like to keep trying but now I can't see any other thing to do but send you there for a while so here's a card with the room number and your name on it. Give it to the teacher (or aide) who is there. I'll give him a call and he'll be expecting you. When you get there he'll explain what he does. As soon as I get some free time later today, I'll come there and talk with you some more. I think you'll like him. He's not going to punish you. He's going to do everything he can to get you back into this class as soon as possible. I'm going to work with him because I want you back."

At this point Tom might say, "I'm sorry, I'll be good, Give me another chance."

Whether you do or not is completely up to you; you know Tom better than anyone else. But suppose you've given him a lot of chances and this is it. Tell him, "No, Tom, please go to the room. No one's going to punish you there and I think you can get some help to work out what seems to be bothering you."

As soon as he leaves, ask the class if they have any suggestions as to what else you could have done that might have allowed you to keep Tom in the room and still teach. As stated, this is a good teaching moment for a little more choice theory instruction by telling them that Tom had choices that didn't involve punishment or more work yet he chose to keep humming. When he comes back, you'll still try to help him and he'll still have choices. But this room is for any student who won't stop disrupting. From Tom's standpoint it may not be a very good place to go but it's the best you can come up with and continue teaching the class.

If they have a good idea, consider it. If this is the first time you've sent a student to The Connecting Place, they may have some questions about the room and why it's called that. Answer them patiently. The more they know why you do things, the better they'll relate to you.

You might tell them that as soon as Tom gets back, they can ask him what went on in The Connecting Place. This will give Tom some attention and give it to him in a way that it doesn't cause trouble. You might also say, that the teacher there will be glad to come to the class and explain what goes on in the room if they want him to do this.

Let's call the person who runs the room, Terry. It would be best if you could have a person who doesn't mind being called by his or her first name. If Tom can call him Terry, it will make Terry's connecting job a lot easier. Terry need not be a teacher or counselor. If money is short, he can be an aide but he should have some training in the choice theory that sets the tone for the room.

There are a lot of mature men and women who are thinking of changing careers and going into education. Recruiting one of these people as he or she takes his or her training might be a possibility. The person needs to be caring, friendly and non-punitive, someone who will not use the seven deadly habits with any student sent to the room. But also it should be a person who can take direction from you, the teacher, who is sending students to the room. You are in charge.

The Connecting Place is my answer to the question, "What do I do with a student who won't let me teach?" that all teachers have been asking me since 1956, when I first began to work in a school. The Connecting Place staffed by someone who knows some choice theory is a good answer because it is directed at solving the problem, not just prolonging it or increasing it as punishment does now.

Let's say that there are six students in the room when Tom arrives. Terry might introduce him to the students and then, with the other six students listening for any differences between what Terry told them and what he tells Tom, both Terry and Tom will have an attentive audience. There should be few differences but, if there are, Terry should be able to explain why. But what Terry says is up to Terry, it is not up to them.

He might start in by saying in a friendly tone of voice, "Tom, I'm glad to have the opportunity to meet you. The Connecting Place rules are simple, stay here with me and we'll have a talk. If you want, do some schoolwork. You can go back to your class when your teacher agrees to take you back. Besides talking with me, what else would you like to do while you're here?"

"What do I have to do?"

"There's nothing you have to do. All we ask is that you be here. If you want to talk, you can talk. You can sit here and think, you really don't have to leave. You can stay here for weeks if it takes us that much time to work out the problem. We have some books for you to read, and you can do your work so you don't get too far behind. Do you have any questions?"

"Yeah, how do I get out of here? I don't want to spend another day in here."

"Getting out of here isn't entirely up to me. It's up to you and the teacher who sent you here. But I'll be happy to talk with you and try to explain why the room is called The Connecting Place. If you can't figure out a way to get along with her, you may be here a long time. I'm willing to talk with you about anything you want to talk about. I'm not bad at tutoring. I'll try to help you if you want some help with your schoolwork."

"But you have to tell her something. How will she know what I'm doing in here if you don't tell her? Like how I'm behaving. Like if I'm good. Don't you give her a report on me?"

"No, I don't do that. That's your job. If you want to, you can write down what you do here. Like this afternoon, you could write down what you did. If what you write is the truth, I'll give it to your teacher when she comes by. I'm sure she'll want to talk with you before you go home even if it's only for a few minutes."

"But what if I don't tell the truth?"

"Then I won't give it to her. I'll give her the truth or nothing at all. I have no intention of saying anything bad about you. I want to be your friend. Friends don't say bad things about each other. Ask the other students if I say anything bad about them. If you say something bad about yourself, well I'd advise you not to, but I won't show it to her unless you want me to."

"But if she doesn't get any report, she'll figure it's bad."

"No, you'll have a chance to talk to her. Of course you can write down some good things you actually did and that way you won't take any chances."

"But she may not let me out of here?"

"All I can tell you is she wants to get along with you better and she wants you to stop what you've been doing in her class so you can come back. But look, I'd like to get along well with you, too. My job is to help you and I'll do all I can. Tom, no one wants to hurt you. We all want you to do well in this school. And this is all we're going to do. We're not going to punish you. It won't hurt any more to sit here than anywhere else in this school. School's important. You've got the brains to do the work. I don't know what else to tell you."

"But my other classes. I'm missing them, too."

"That's up to your other teachers. They know you're here. If they want you to come to their class tomorrow, they can send for you. I hope they do."

Every student who acts out in class knows how to behave. In a GQS all you're asking is they behave well enough so you can teach and others can learn. It's not Terry's job to tell them what to do to get back into their class or classes but he did give Tom some good advice. There are no threats or punishment in The Connecting Place assuming that what Tom does isn't against the law. The same policy applies in The Connecting Place as in the school for violence or threats of violence. Parents would be contacted and the student taken home immediately or into custody as in the case of any student who seriously breaks the law.

Tom knows what to do. It's his job to figure out if he wants to do it, and then, when he gets back to class, do it. Teachers don't want to get involved in a back and forth game between the class and The Connecting

Place. The important aspect of The Connecting Place is that it accomplishes what it is designed to do: help students like Tom trust teachers enough to connect with them.

The Connecting Place is a new and very puzzling situation for students like Tom. In the external control schools they are used to, students like Tom who can scrape along with D's, had the upper hand. They could get a lot of attention by engaging in small wars against their teachers and blame all the punishment they suffered as a good reason for continuing their rebellious behavior.

The teachers in those schools had no escape from these students if they were clever enough not to go too far. Rebellious kids even have the silent support of a lot of students who also hate the external control system but accept it better than Tom. He can sense that support and also use it as an excuse to disrupt. Teaching in tough schools, for many teachers, is like a war. In a GQS with the CBC and circle-ups plus The Connecting Place, the war is over.

When the teacher who sent Tom to The Connecting Place comes to see him, he'll want to go back to class. What follows is an imaginary conversation between Tom and her. Imagine you are she.

"Tom, I got out of my last period class for a few minutes so I could get to see you before school ends. How've you been doing in here?"

"It sucks, all we do is sit here."

"I sent you some work, to read a chapter in the history book, did you read it?"

"You said I didn't have to do any work if I didn't want to."

"That's right. You don't have to do it. I was just hoping you would. Did you read it?"

"I read it. It was better than just sitting here. Besides Jerry helped me with it. Can I come back to your class? I hate being stuck in here."

"I hate having you here. That's why I'm here to talk with you. What'll you do if you come back to class tomorrow?"

"I won't hum anymore. I'm sorry about that."

"Tom, it helped you that Jerry worked with you on that chapter, didn't it?"

"He's a nice guy. I gave him a hard time for while but it didn't seem to bother him."

"But it helped you?"

"Yeah, it helped me."

"Would you like some help with the next chapter when you get back to class?"

"What do you mean? I don't need any help."

"I mean I talked to your team and they all want to help you. I'd like you to give it a chance."

Here the key is to get Tom to accept some help. His team had given up on him because he didn't want to accept help and they knew he needed it. He's afraid to ask for help because that will hurt his tough guy image in class. No one saw him get help from Jerry. Jerry can deal with the hard time Tom gave him. His team has no patience for that kind of behavior. He's still thinking about you saying that he needs some help.

You could say, "The idea of getting help bothers you doesn't it? You're smart enough, with a little help you could make a B."

"You'll never give me a B. When you explained all that stuff about no low grades I didn't believe a word you said."

"Have I lied to you about no punishment? Is there anything else I could have done besides send you here? Has Jerry punished you?"

"No, it's been okay. I just don't like being here."

"I asked you why you think I'd lie to you about no more low grades. Do you think I'm trying to trick you into doing schoolwork?"

"You'd really give me a B if I did some work?"

"Not some work, B work. But you can get all the help you need. I'll even help you if you'll let me."

"But I've been giving you a hard time for a month since school started. Why would you want to help me?"

"I'm a teacher. My job is to help you learn. When I can't help a kid I give myself a low grade. I'm flunking with you, Tom. I don't like it."

"I guess I can come back."

"I guess you can."

I wanted to show you how to talk to a student like Tom. In the Schwab School in Cincinnati we had hundreds of student like Tom. I didn't want to end up with a low grade for all my work that year. This conversation is typical of how we reached the kids there. I have never before worked in a school that was more dysfunctional than Schwab. Unfortunately, the Cincinnati Public School District decided to abandon all we started so Schwab can no longer be seen as we left it but what happened as described in Chapter Ten in the book *Choice Theory* is an understatement of how well these ideas worked there.

Dealing with the students who are still connected but who are engaging in incidents that are harmful to the school.

In order to prevent more students from becoming problem students like Tom, I suggest you consider the following from Dave Dyment, the Principal of the Mill Plain Elementary School, Evergreen School District, Vancouver, Washington. Dave has completed training in the Glasser Quality School ideas and is an instructor in the William Glasser Institute, doing training in his spare time away from school and, of course, working with his own staff. While his school is involved in competence based education, he, his staff and his parent body have not yet declared Mill Plain to be a GQS. But they are close. When I told him I was writing this book, he wrote to me and the following is a portion of his letter:

> Two years ago, we implemented a program called *The Choice Program*. The Choice Program starts with every relationship in the building. Since we have 750 students, 45 teachers, 12 classified staff and approximately 1000 parents, we have a significant number of relationship dynamics which are constantly in motion. Our Choice Program is built upon the principle that the quality of the relationships in our school is the most important factor. We don't take lightly how relationships drive our behavior and don't take good relationships for granted. The morale on staff is very high most of the time and the staff is very special to one another. Our children are loved and our parents hold the school in

high esteem. We continually attempt to do things that build relationships and we do our best to not behave in ways that will damage the relationships that we've taken the time to build.

One of the focal points of our choice program is a tool used to teach problem solving skills and avoid power struggles between children and adults or children and other students. Since our school was big enough to qualify for an assistant principal, I approached my supervisor, Becky Fleming, and explored an alternative system. The system, even with adding another administrator, was just not working. The assistant principal simply helped to break up fights and suspend kids.

As the principal, I was the teachers' last resort and a lot of problems from school buses, playground or classrooms would end up on my desk. All were power struggles between a child and an adult or between children. The child had acted out for a variety of reasons and usually while angry had tangled with a bus driver, teacher or other students. These power struggles are relationship killers and prevent our system from moving toward the quality relationships we wanted in the school.

Brain storming with my boss, Becky Fleming, a true lead manager, resulted in an alternative system based on improving relationships and reducing power struggles. The conference with Becky resulted in the hiring of additional staff assistant time instead of the assistant principal.

These two people joined three other staff assistants (basically trained aides) already on board for a five member team that operated our Choice Room.

These five staff assistants were all hired with choice theory in mind and were given a basic intensive week of training in the Glasser choice theory concepts as they related to improving school relationships. These five people are naturals at the use of choice theory and are experts at maintaining relationships with children while using effective problem solving strategies.

Children are taught usable techniques in problem solving based on the concept of choice theory and use "angering" behaviors much less frequently. These problems are worked on away from the classrooms and buses where the problem started. Teachers and bus drivers recognize that when a person has a problem, the problem needs to be dealt with and solved so that they can get down to the business of doing what they are hired to do. Children may also choose to go to the Choice Room for assistance and do so frequently.

The following belief statement about problem solving is posted in all rooms in our school: *At Mill Plain, we believe, that when we have a problem, we sit down and work it out.* We attempt to practice this at all levels in our system but it is most visible in our Choice Room.

The result of this system change has been remarkable. Teachers and bus drivers finally have a tool which allows children to work out problems. Problems often get solved before power struggles occur, and before relationships are destroyed. With good relationships driving our program, the joy and happiness that make up the Quality School has finally been able to flourish.

Certainly these five people who have provided such a wonderful change to our system are not the whole program. The whole program cannot be summed up in this letter. There is a lot more so if you want to learn more about what we're doing in our little school give the institute a call. I am very proud of this school and would love to share it with any of the readers of your book.

If you would like to read other research documented information about using Glasser Quality School ideas in other schools, refer to Wubbolding, *Reality Therapy for the 21st Century*. This new, comprehensive and definitive book is well worth reading.

Twelve

The Role of the Principal in a Glasser Quality School

I have had the opportunity to meet many great principals including the men and women who have led their schools to become the first Glasser Quality Schools in the world. But even before I conceived of the Quality School idea, I was involved with a few schools that could have easily met almost all the criteria for a Quality School rating as noted in the first chapter of this book. I say *almost all the criteria* because I had not yet developed choice theory so it could not be taught to the students. But they did use and teach reality therapy, an important precursor of choice theory.

Two school leaders, whom I worked with in the sixties, were so outstanding that what I learned from them forty years ago has become a cornerstone of my ideas on education. The first, whom I worked with until he retired, is Donald O'Donnell, the principal of the first *School Without Failure*, the Ventura Elementary School in Palo Alto, California. It was from Don that I learned that the best school is a joyful school.

The second was Beatrice Dolan, the Superintendent of the Ventura School for Girls in Ventura, California. From her I learned that every student can succeed in school. It is a complete coincidence that these schools had the same name. But it is not a coincidence that they were both *Schools Without Failure*. In fact, as stated in Chapter Four, it was while I was working with Bea Dolan at the Ventura Girls School that I first became acquainted with what has been a driving force in my work with schools: eliminating failure from your school.

I am addressing this chapter to principals because of what I first learned from Don and Bea: Unless the principal leads the way, there will be no major change for the better in any school. But the word *leads* is crucial. A leader is someone you follow because you want to follow, because his or her leadership helps you to do your job more effectively and enjoyably. Every GQS has such a principal and, if it is to continue after the first principal retires, it will need the same leadership from the next principal. You are crucial to the process.

Last night, when I was awake in the middle of the night, I began to put together what to write in this chapter. When I thought about the principals of the first Glasser Quality Schools I asked myself, "Should I attempt to describe what they do so you could learn from them?" But I decided against it. Each one of them did and does what he or she thinks is the best thing to do in their school at the time. They learned some basics from me but they figured out the rest themselves. They may all be Quality Schools but no two are the same. Copying is not the way to a GQS. I suggest if you visit, it should be more to assure you the job can be done rather than to look for the recipe for doing it.

When I was very young, about seven years old, my father used to take me with him when he went to the office on Saturday or Sunday to meet with salesmen trying to sell him some goods for his business. I was puzzled by the fact that although they were all salesmen, they were so different in personality, language and dress. Finally, I asked my Dad about it and he answered, "They aren't nearly as different as they seem. One thing they have in common: they all want to sell."

When I think of our GQS principals and even Dave Dyment who's close to getting there—his letter is quoted in Chapter Eleven—they are also very different in personality and how they approach people. But three things are the same. They are all trying to replace external control with choice theory, all working to stamp out low grades and failure and all leading the way to joy in their schools.

If I were to try to describe them as individuals, most of the words I would have to use would describe a person who has stopped using the deadly habits and replaced them with words that exemplify their move to the connecting habits. They have also figured out many ways on their own to take their schools to the place they are now. In fact, I think you can read between the lines of Dave Dyment's letter and feel how deeply involved he is in what he's doing. The fact he is so anxious to share his considerable success bears this out.

If you read this book and then begin to make the effort to do what these people have done, you are the same kind of leader they are. If I can reach people like you, there will soon be far more than eight Glasser Quality Schools. I don't feel adequate to write any more about the kind of people you are. I get emotional when I think of what you and your teachers will be attempting to do. Literally, you will be saving lives that would otherwise be lost.

If you are such a principal, you, your staff, your students and their parents know who you are. I also believe many of the ideas in this book are not that new to you. Anyone who loves young people thinks in a similar vein. Even if you are just starting out, I will be honored to make your acquaintance and willing to do all I can to help you. My number is in this book, I welcome your call. What I would enjoy doing is to make an audiotape that you and your staff can share. Send me your questions.

Last night just before I went back to sleep, as I was thinking how to write this chapter, my mind wandered back to my early days with Don O'Donnell and Bea Dolan. I kept thinking, what exactly did they do that so captured me at the time and has held me captive ever since? I'm not even sure they knew what it was and, at the time, I didn't either.

All I knew was something about them struck me and continues to hold me as I struggle in this book to express as much as I can to help you. Whatever it was, if I could put it into words, it might be able to do a little more for you and your teachers than I've done so far. As I continued to think, something popped into my mind.

What both Don and Bea projected was trust. I felt safe when I was with them in their school. I could also see their staff felt the same way. For me it was the safety to make suggestions, talk to the staff, talk to the students and never feel as if I had to worry about anything. I was free to do my work even though, much of the time I worked in their schools, I didn't always know what I was doing. But in the safe, trusting environment they created, I was not upset about not even knowing what I didn't know. From them I got the courage to go ahead and do much of what I've done. Courage is important, the safer your school, the more courage your teachers will have.

I feel safe in writing all I've written because, as I said early in this book, by now I'm sure there is no downside to what I'm suggesting. Even if all you as a principal or teacher can do is sit with a student like Tom and tell him, "I don't know what to do, but somehow you and I have to become friends. You may not think so but I'm on your side. Just relax, Tom, and talk with me."

It's that safety thing. Telling a student that no one here is going to hurt you is such a contrast to what students have experienced in external control schools where even the good students and good teachers don't really feel safe from criticism. When I say safe, I'm talking about mental safety, a state of mind, that allows a principal, a teacher or a student to feel free to express their feelings without worrying that they have to act on the same feelings. But it can go even further than that for both teachers and students if they are sure you, as their principal, are not only going to stop using the deadly habits, you have banished them from your mind.

Minus the habits, in the Quality Schools I've visited, staff members corner me and tell me what they are doing in the school almost as if they feel you, the principal, want them to go beyond where they are, to begin to think and feel in new ways. I think for many of your students, the school can be the best place in their lives. I mean not only for elementary students but for middle school and high school students, too.

I recommend you, literally, send your teachers the message that Bea and Don sent me: We have an almost impossible job if our goal is for all students to succeed. I don't think we can reach that goal if you don't feel free to tap every neuronal link in your brain—all four hundred billion of them—to figure out how we can connect with all these students, especially, when so many have been disconnected from teachers and schoolwork for years.

As you try to lead your staff away from external control and toward choice theory, you will be doubly tested. The first test will be from staff members who want to stay with external control and don't believe you really want to leave it. They'll keep dragging their feet and waiting to see what you're going to do. The second test will be from the staff members who want to go much faster than is possible and will blame you for dragging your feet.

But what both groups are doing, even though I don't believe either group is aware they are doing it, is testing your connection with them, testing whether you will fall back to using the deadly habits when problems arise. It's an easy test to flunk. To pass it, you have to keep saying to the teachers in both groups, "I want all of us, to give up external control. But I recognize I can only control myself so I'm going to stop using it. There is nothing else I know to do if we are to move our school to the point where all students succeed."

They will keep watching you to see if you do what you say. The students will watch the teachers the same way the teachers will watch you. If you can pass your teachers' test, your teachers will be able to pass their students' test.

All the while, don't count on many people to help you. Whenever you try anything new in your school, especially as new as all students succeeding, the schools around you will not be very supportive. They know that if you succeed there will be pressure on them to do the same thing. But the main thing is the pressure should never come from you. Offer to help, to let schools visit but don't tell them it's something they need to do. You are not doing this to be better than other schools; you are doing it for your students and because you believe in it. If you study history and science, you will find that the world is not a friendly place for people who walk down the uncharted pathways.

In 1990, when Bea Dolan was over ninety years old, we invited her to come to Cincinnati for the twenty-fifth year anniversary of the reality therapy that actually was born in the Ventura School For girls when she was superintendent. At the last minute she got quite ill and could not come but she did have the strength to write us a letter. In it she said, "We worked so hard but we finally did what needed so much to be done. And in the end what did we have for all we did? *We had each other*."

Endnotes

[1] Breggin, Peter, M.D. (1998). *Talking Back To Ritalin.* Common Courage Press (www/breggin.com/prbbooks.html).

[2] Op. cit.

[3] The Transition Year Support Team is situated at: Blackrock Education Centre, Kill Avenue, Dun Laoghaire, County Dublin, Ireland, Telephone +353 1 2301671, fax +353 1 2301612, E-mail transit@indigo.ie

[4] David Grissmer of the Rand Corporation in a study of national school performance published in *The Los Angeles Times* 7-26-00.

[5] Judy Clap's ideas are expanded upon in her two books listed in the Annotated Bibliography, Appendix C.

[6] This material has been expanded in Linda McNeil's recent book noted in the Annotated Bibliography, Appendix C.

[7] Resnick, Michael D., PhD, et al. "Protecting Adolescents From Harm", JAMA, September 10, 1997.

Appendix A

The Glasser Quality Schools as of October 2001

Aikman Elementary School
Charles Lyles, Principal
900 Avenue K, Hereford, TX 79045
Phone: 806-363-7640, Fax: 806-363-7699
E-mail: charleslyles@hisd.net

Belleair Montessori Academy
Joan Kirk, Head Directress
905 Ponce de Leon Boulevard, Clearwater, FL 33756
Phone: 727-584-2867, Fax: 727-559-8416
E-mail: gatorbate78@cs.com

Canterbury High School
Diann Causey, Principal
312 Chisholm St., Montgomery, AL 36110
Phone: 334-834-2273, Fax: 334-834-5782
E-mail: firstqualityhs@aol.com

Horizons K-8 Alternative School
Ann Kane, Lead-Teacher
4545 Sioux Drive, Boulder, CO 80303
Phone: 303-447-5580, Fax: 303-447-5580
E-mail: ann.kane@admin.bvsd.k12.co.us

Murray High School
Vicki Miller, Principal
Charlotte Wellen, Contact
1200 Forest Street, Charlottesville, VA 22903
Phone: 804-296-3090, Fax: 804-979-6479
E-mail: wellen1@earthlink.net

Huntington Woods Elementary School
Andrea van der Laan, Principal
4334 Byron Center S.W., Wyoming, MI 49509
Phone: 616-530-7537, Fax: 616-249-7656
E-mail: avdl@aol.com

LABBB Collaborative Programs
Robert Renna, Director
251 Waltham Street/House J, Lexington, MA 02421
Phone: 781-861-2400, Fax: 781-861-1351
E-mail: quality2@juno.com

McFall Elementary School
Bill Rich, Principal
509 W. Main, Middleville, MI 49333
Phone: 616-795-3637, Fax: 616-795-5554
E-mail: mcfallelementary@tk.k12.mi.us

Beaverbrook School
Janet Longaphie, Principal
1085 Mountain Road, Moncton, N.B. E1B 2P2, Canada
Fax: 506-856-3605
E-mail: longajah@nbed.nb.ca

Charyl Stockwell Academy
(formerly Livingston Developmental Academy)
Diane Vance, Principal
9758 East Highland Road, Howell, MI 48843
Phone: 810-632-2200, Fax: 810-632-2201
E-mail: dvance@1daschool.com
Website: www.1daschool.com

Appendix B

The William Glasser Institute

In 1967, I founded the Institute for Reality Therapy for the purpose of teaching that therapy. The Institute is a nonprofit, charitable foundation. Neither my wife, Carleen, nor I take any salary for our work at the Institute. Since its inception, I have greatly expanded my thinking with the addition of choice theory and have applied that theory to almost every aspect of reality therapy. I have also extended the use of choice theory into the schools, as exemplified by the quality school, and into managing for quality in all other areas in which people are managed. My ideas are being applied to an entire community in Corning, New York.

With all these expansions and applications, I have gone so far beyond reality therapy that, for accuracy, I was encouraged to change the name of the Institute to the William Glasser Institute. I made the change so that anyone who is interested in any of my ideas and of my applications of these ideas could easily contact us. Over the years, as our teaching and training have expanded, satellite institutes have been set up in many countries around the world.

The Institute serves the public through its membership and benefits its members in many ways. Membership is an acknowledgment of a commitment to the principles and practices of reality therapy, lead management, and choice theory psychology. The

Institute coordinates and monitors all training programs and serves as an information clearing house. My latest thinking is often made available through audiotapes, videotapes, and publications. As a networking center, people can exchange ideas through the Institute's newsletter and connect through international conventions and regional meetings. The Institute lends support to its members in their work with individuals, agencies, and communities. The *International Journal of Reality Therapy* published out of Northeastern University is a vehicle through which members can publish their works on new ways of using and teaching reality therapy. The Institute also provides a voice for the membership through regional representatives and international liaisons.

The basic effort of the William Glasser Institute centers on an intensive educational training program for individual professionals who want to use my ideas in their work with others. This training is also offered as part of the program for schools to become a Glasser Quality School. There are five parts to this training, which takes a minimum of eighteen months to complete: first, a Basic Intensive Week, which is available to small groups, with no more than 13-16 participants per instructor; a Basic Practicum for a minimum of thirty hours; an Advanced Intensive Week with a different instructor; and following that, an Advanced Practicum. Finally, at the recommendation of the supervisor of the Advanced Practicum, a trainee attends a Certification Week and demonstrates what he or she has learned. For this demonstration, the Institute gives a certificate of completion. This certificate is not a license to practice, but the training is often used to obtain college credit and continuing education units.

Right now there are more that 5,600 certificate holders worldwide.

After obtaining Reality Therapy Certification, some trainees opt to go on with their training and become instructors in our organization. There are four levels of instructors: The Basic Practicum Supervisor who can teach a Basic Practicum; the Advanced Practicum Supervisor who can teach both Basic and Advanced Practica; the Basic Week Instructor who can teach both practica, as well as the Basic Intensive Week; and the Advanced Week Instructor who can teach all four phases.

The Glasser Quality School Training Program is a program based on the concepts first described in my book, *The Quality School*, and later in *Choice Theory: A New Psychology of Personal Freedom*. The program is geared towards helping individual schools create the necessary systemic change that can lead to the creation of a Glasser Quality School. In this process, the role of the principal, utilizing lead-management principles, is crucial to the process. Once the staff is committed to the vision of creating such a school and has begun to facilitate change in the school structure, intensive week training is provided.

Fees for this training are paid by the schools, but schools that don't have the funding usually apply and get funding from a variety of sources. Since a quality school is a drug-free school, federal and state grants may be available through drug-prevention funds. If a committed school puts effort into it, the funding can usually be obtained. Each phase is funded separately, so the initial outlay may be within the training budget of many schools.

All our instruction is by explanation and demonstration. These are *hands-on* programs. It is our hope that people will contact the William Glasser Institute and find out how we can help anyone, any group, any school, or any community to pursue these ideas.

The Institute employs user-friendly, choice-theory-trained people, so if you contact us, you can be sure of a courteous response. It is my vision to teach choice theory to the world. I invite you to join me in this effort.

For further information about my work, lectures, books, and audio and video materials as well as the Institute programs, contact:

The William Glasser Institute
22024 Lassen Street, Suite 118
Chatsworth, CA 91311
Phone: 800-899-0688
Fax: 818-700-0555
Email: wginst@earthlink.net
Web: www.wglasser.com

Appendix C

Annotated Bibliography

Breggin, Peter, M.D. (1998) *Talking Back To Ritalin*, Common Courage Press (www/breggin.com /prbbooks,html). Details the side effects and potential problems with Ritalin and other stimulants, and offers advice for parents and other adults on how to help children without resorting to psychiatric drugs.

Brickell, J., and Wubbolding, R. (1999) *Counseling with Reality Therapy*. London: Winslow Press (513-561-1911). Choice Theory in the context of school counseling containing application to both substance abuse and stages of group development.

Buck, N. (2000) *Peaceful Parenting*. Black Forest Press San Diego, California (www.peaceful parenting.com). This book helps parents learn ways to provide a safe, healthy environment that supports the goal of teaching children to meet their own needs in responsible ways. The result is an improved quality of life for the family where loving relationships are developed and maintained.

Claps, J. (2000), *Making the Parent Connection*, Philadelphia: Songhai Press Corp. (1-877-SONGHAI). Suggestions for parents and teachers which incorporate the essential ingredients for building successful parent-teacher-student partnership to ensure quality education in our schools.

Claps, J. (1984), *Rap It Up, Hellertown*, PA: J.B. Claps & Associates (610-346-7629). A step by step guide on how to conduct successful classroom discussions including sample discussion topics and questions.

Crawford, Bodine & Hoglund (1993), *The School for Quality Learning: Managing the School and Classroom the Deming Way*. Champaign, IL: Research Press. Bob Hoglund Center for Quality Education, Inc. (480) 839-7855 or www.cqeinc.com. The information in this book leads the reader from theory to practice: understanding quality as the solution; managing the school for quality learning; managing the classroom for quality learning.

Glasser, Carleen, M.Ed. (1998), The Quality World Series. Los Angeles: The William Glasser Institute, (800-899-0688). Versions are available for early childhood education, elementary school, and middle school. Teaching aids to help students learn responsible behavior, internal motivation, problem solving, conflict resolution, and choices that help them.

Glasser, W., M.D. (2001), *Counseling With Choice Theory, The NewReality Therapy,* formerly titled *Reality Therapy In Action*. Los Angeles: The William Glasser Institute, (800-899-0688). The expanded, clarified, updated version of Reality Therapy. Dr. Glasser invites the reader to sit with him while he counsels a variety of clients and reveals the explicit core of his counseling method, sharing his thoughts as the counseling proceeds.

Glasser, W., M.D. (1998), *Choice Theory, A New Psychology of Personal Freedom*. Los Angeles: The William Glasser Institute, (800-899-0688). The basic theory for all Dr. Glasser's work, choice theory is a noncontrolling psychology that gives us the freedom to sustain the relationships that lead to healthy, productive lives.

Glasser, W., M.D. and Glasser, Carleen, M.Ed. (1998), *The Language of Choice Theory*. Los Angeles: The William Glasser Institute, (800-899-0688). Special examples of how to use choice theory language in parenting, marriage, school, and work; imagined typical conversations in real-life situations comparing controlling or threatening responses with those using choice theory.

Glasser, W., M.D. (1998), *Choice Theory in the Classroom*. Los Angeles: The William Glasser Institute, (800-899-0688). This book translates choice theory into a productive, classroom model of team learning with emphasis on satisfaction and excitement.

Glasser, W., M.D. (1998), *The Quality School, Managing Students Without Coercion*. Los Angeles: The William Glasser Institute, (800-899-0688). Develops the concept of a Quality School where there is no failure because all students are doing competent work and many are doing quality work.

Glasser, W., M.D. (1998), *The Quality School Teacher*. Los Angeles: The William Glasser Institute, (800-899-0688). Follow up and companion volume to *The Quality School*, based on the work of W. E. Deming and Dr. Glasser's choice theory and written for teachers trying to abandon the old system of boss-managing for lead-management.

Glasser, W., M.D. (1969), *Schools without Failure*. Los Angeles: The William Glasser Institute, (800-899-0688). Details the shortcomings of current education and proposes a daring new program to reduce school failure — a program based on increased involvement, relevance, and thinking.

Greene, B. (1998) *Self-Esteem and the Quality School*, Kings Beach, CA: Brad Greene (530-546-5550). The story of one high school's journey to quality using Dr. William Glasser's concepts of Choice Theory.

Greene, B. (1994) *New Paradigms for Creating Quality Schools*, Kings Beach, CA: Brad Greene (530-546-5550). Dr. William Glasser's concepts of Choice Theory used in classroom situations as well as examples of schools using these ideas.

Ludwig, Sally A., and Kaye W. Mentley (1997) *Quality is the Key: Stories from Huntington Woods School*, KWM Educational Services, Inc. (E-mail: kwmedserv@aol.com). This account of Huntington Woods Elementary, the first Quality School, describes the ways that Dr. Glasser's ideas were brought to life from the design stage to the present. A useful, practical guide for educators and parents.

McNeil, Linda (2000) *Contradictions of School Reform:Educational Costs of Standardized Testing*, Critical Social Thought Series: Routledge, N.Y. Linda McNeil's meticulous research documents the harm inflicted on both student achievement and teacher motivation when schools are driven by the standardized achievement tests now used in almost all states.

Palmatier, L., Ed.D. (1998) *Crisis Counseling for a Quality School Community.* Bristol, Penn., Accelerated Development. The late Larry Palmatier has provided a comprehensive guide for counseling students who choose out-of-control behaviors. Substance abuse, depression, sexual abuse, gangs, grief and conflict resolution are among the pressing issues dealt with from the point of reality therapy.

Suffield, Jean Seville (1998) *Conflict Resolution: Creating a Learning Environment.* Quebec (Canada): Jean Seville (450) 446-5671; seville@total.net. "Tried & true" activities by teachers for teachers that help create a warm and friendly need-filling learning environment and plan with students ways for effectively dealing with their lives.

Suffield, Jean Seville (1999) *Action...take 1: Self-Evaluation & the Student-Led Conference.* Quebec (Canada): Jean Seville (450) 446-5671; seville@total.net. Activities based on Choice Theory and Quality School concepts that help students self-evaluate, take ownership for their own learning and communicate that learning through student-led parent conferencing.

Sullo, R. (1993) *Teach Them To Be Happy.* To order, contact Bob Sullo (508-888-7627). Designed to teach Choice theory to parents and teachers of children from pre-school through the mid-elementary grades.

Includes numerous activities that can be used both in school and at home.

Sullo, R. (1997) *Inspiring Quality in Your School: From Theory to Practice.* To order, contact Bob Sullo (508-888-7627). A valuable companion to Dr. Glasser's *The Quality School.* Provides specific steps to guide individual teachers and entire faculties taking the journey to quality.

Sullo, R. (1999) *The Inspiring Teacher: New Beginnings for the 21st Century.* To order, contact Bob Sullo (508-888-7627). Especially well suited for teachers interested in bringing together the ideas of choice theory and the principles of brain-based learning. Helps teachers develop a clear picture and action plan as they move toward inspiring more students.

Wubbolding, R. (1994) *Reality Therapy with Children.* Cincinnati, OH: Center for Reality Therapy (513-561-1911). Structured approach for talking with children in a non-coercive, nurturing and positive manner illustrating productive conferencing skills.

Wubbolding, R. (2000) *Reality Therapy for the 21st Century.* Philadelphia, PA: Brunner-Routledge (513-561-1911). Immediately useable skills and techniques highlighting lead management and cross-cultural applications, and answering questions about research supporting the effectiveness of quality schools.

Index